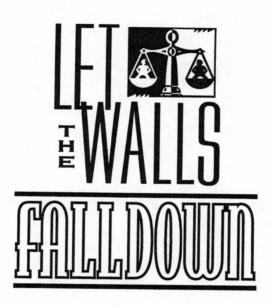

LET THE WALLS FALL DOWN

LET THE WALLS

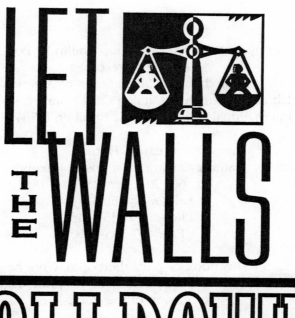

FALL DOWN

PHILLIP PORTER

CREATION HOUSE
BOOKS ABOUT SPIRIT-LED LIVING • ORLANDO, FLORIDA

Creation House
Strang Communications Company
600 Rinehart Road
Lake Mary, FL 32746
Phone: 407-333-3132
Fax: 407-333-7100

Dedicated to the memory of the late Pastor and Mrs. Phillip H. Porter, Sr, my mom and dad

ACKNOWLEDGMENTS

To my lovely wife, Edgar Lee Moye Porter, for her thirty-nine years of faithful encouragement and belief in me.

To my children, Phillip III, Katherine, Stephen, Arthur, Denise, Phyllis, Terrance and Elijah, for their undying faith and belief in their dad.

To Terry Whalin, who without his help and friendship, this book would have never been. Thank you, Terry.

To Dr. Marilyn Chipman, Katherine Porter, Marilyn Hill and Arthur Porter, who all helped in the final preparation of this book.

To my brothers and sisters, Geraldine Meeks, Shirley Morris, Thomas M. Porter, Sandra Toles, Vera Porter, Russel M. Porter, Nettie Watkins, Lois Tunnstall and Michael Porter, who first took me through the process of reconciling differences.

To the members of All Nations Pentecostal Center Church of God in Christ in Aurora/Denver for their sharing me with so many other groups and the world at large.

For Promise Keepers and the opportunity they've given me to serve them and their companions as chairman of the board of directors.

To Bill McCartney, Randy Phillips, Gordon England, Rick Kingham, Dick Blair, George McKinney, Tom Porter, Hank Peters, Sid Overton and Dick Clark, who have helped to keep me accountable.

To Stephen Strang and Creation House for their faith that I had a book in me.

For the Montana Jurisdiction Church of God in Christ, whom I serve with great joy.

CONTENTS

FOREWORD

Throughout my daily rituals of life, I tend to run into diverse kinds of individuals. It's not that these people are unusual or eccentric — they are simply different from me. These people look and act differently than me.

I am used to the way my life runs its course. I see the world in a certain light. But Bishop Phillip Porter sees the world in a completely different way. As a black man, he does not experience things the way I do as a white man. By the same token, as a white man I will never know what it is like to live in this world as a black man. We are different.

More than ever I believe God has raised up Promise Keepers to call men to cross racial and denominational barriers and demonstrate biblical unity. Thankfully, the Lord brought Bishop into my life, who would not only change my perspective toward my brothers in Christ, but who would also provide for me leadership and accountability.

Phillip Porter is the perfect choice as chairman of the board of directors for Promise Keepers. His wisdom, love, experience, maturity and track record are extraordinary. Appropriately, the 1996 theme for Promise Keepers is Break Down the Walls. We are calling men to break down the walls by becoming ambassadors of reconciliation (2 Cor. 5:18-21).

In order to break down the walls, we need God's Spirit to strike a revival in our hearts. We must be reconciled to God, then to our families and ultimately to our brothers in Christ. Bishop and I have experienced the brokenness that comes with reconciliation. It has been my privilege to spend time with this man of God and to experience his passion for revival and reconciliation.

In this book Bishop will kindle a fire within you to reach out to people who are different from you. He won't just tell you how his life has changed since God did the work of reconciliation within him, but he will show you through personal accounts. You will have the privilege of knowing and learning from a man whom God has gifted with the ability to see beyond all barriers.

Although Bishop and I are different in many

ways, we have begun to break down the walls and see each other with the mind of Christ. Remember, man looks on the outward appearance, but it is God who looks on the heart. By laying down our lives and hungering for God's will, we will let the walls fall down.

Bill McCartney
Founder of Promise Keepers

THERE IS WITHIN EVERYONE OF US
A LONGING TO DO OUR PART
TO BE ONE WITH GOD
AND ONE WITH EACH OTHER.

CHAPTER 1

HOW DARE THEY TALK ABOUT RECONCILIATION!

The August afternoon sun was bright over the Rocky Mountains west of Denver. I sat in my office at the All Nations Pentecostal Center Church of God in Christ in the Denver suburb of Aurora, Colorado, and inside I was seething. In a few minutes, men from the new group called Promise Keepers would arrive at my church.

This meeting was the result of a phone call I received several days earlier from someone at Promise Keepers.

"We're looking for African American leaders to join with us," the man said.

"Fine. Come on down," I answered. This was an unexpected opportunity to speak with Coach Bill McCartney and I welcomed it.

While I didn't know much about Promise Keepers I knew their founder was Coach Bill McCartney from the University of Colorado (CU). In the last few weeks I had been looking for a way to make a strong move *against* Coach McCartney.

Just weeks earlier in July 1990 an African American tailback on the CU Buffaloes, Eric Bieniemy, had been arrested. Allegedly Eric had assaulted an Aurora firefighter at the home of Eric's mother. As a leader in Aurora I was asked to help Eric. Although the season hadn't begun, sportswriters were touting him as a contender for the prestigious Heisman Trophy. It was quite an honor for Eric who grew up in Watts, a poor section of Los Angeles, California, that is infamous for its riots in the 1960s.

Because Eric was suspended, many of us feared the tailback would lose his chance for the Heisman. The nerve of this white coach to jeopardize the chance of a lifetime for this highly motivated kid! It looked to me like Coach McCartney suspended this player because of pressure from the media and the CU alumni.

As I learned more about the events leading to Eric's arrest, I felt the accusations against him had racial undertones. When the fire broke out at his mother's house Eric and other CU players extinguished the blaze. In the middle of the commotion someone in the neighborhood called the fire

17

department and the police. When the firemen arrived, immediately one of them took an ax and tore into the wall of the garage.

"Stop! We've put out the fire," Eric yelled. The fireman continued to damage the wall, so Eric stopped him with what came naturally. He tackled the man. As the two struggled, the police arrived and arrested Bieniemy. Two weeks later Coach McCartney announced that Eric would be suspended for the first CU football game.

I went with Eric for his appearance before Aurora municipal court. He pleaded no contest and was sentenced to forty hours of community service which he performed at All Nations Church, which I pastor. From my perspective Eric's community service and suspension were unnecessary. All I could think about was creating a means to get this white coach's attention, and this meeting with Promise Keepers looked like my perfect opportunity.

Right on schedule several men from Promise Keepers arrived at the church, and we gathered in the basement. To my surprise Coach McCartney was among this group of men. For several minutes I listened patiently as the men explained the overall goals of Promise Keepers and their desire to reach the African American community. They told me about the Seven Promises of a Promise Keeper. In particular they emphasized the sixth promise — to reach beyond any racial and denominational barriers to demonstrate the power of biblical unity.

At that point I decided I had listened long enough to their talk — especially about reconciliation. "The audacity of you to come and talk to us about

18

racial reconciliation when you have acted against an African American," I said to the men. "It's just another case of white men against black."

At first everyone looked bewildered at my response. Finally Coach McCartney asked, "Are you talking about Eric Bieniemy?"

"Yes," I said, "you immediately suspended him without rhyme or reason. It's another case of taking these players and just using them."

"Oh, no," Coach McCartney protested, "you don't understand. I followed a rule we have which suspends anyone who has been arrested or incarcerated. Every player knows these rules, and the rules don't discriminate against blacks."

As the coach was saying this he realized that in many places black players were more likely to be arrested than white players because of their skin color. "Oh, God, it could be wrong," he said. Rising from his seat Coach McCartney got on his knees before me. "I never meant to do anything wrong against my black brothers, and I apologize. And beyond apologizing here in this private meeting, I'll do it publicly."

As Coach McCartney knelt in front of me I started to tug on his sleeve. "Oh, man, get up," I said. A key leader of the Colorado community was kneeling before me, and it felt strange. But he insisted on staying there.

Suddenly I began to feel overwhelmed at the situation. "All right," I said, "at least I'm beginning to understand your reason for suspending Eric."

While Coach McCartney unintentionally committed an act of prejudice I was equally guilty. The Holy

Spirit made me aware that without a second thought, I was prejudiced against his actions. Everybody who is not your color is not your enemy. I automatically believed that this white man was acting prejudicially against blacks. I repented for this, and Coach McCartney forgave my act of prejudice. A spirit of reconciliation fell on the group of men. Our meeting shifted into a discussion about how Promise Keepers could gain the cooperation of the African American community.

"Dr. Porter," the men said, "we want you to serve on the Promise Keepers board." It was hard to believe what I was hearing.

"You don't understand how the African American ministerial alliance functions," I explained. "Pastors can't be selected on their own. The alliance must choose us. Otherwise it's not right."

Several weeks later the African American ministerial alliance met for breakfast. Coach McCartney attended and listened as the ministers talked about the heart of the inner city. When his turn came to address the group Coach Mac, as I now call my friend, was transparent and clear. Eventually the alliance selected two men — Dick Clark, who was a local business owner, and myself — to serve on the fifteen-member Promise Keepers Board of Directors.

During my first year I was elected vice chairman, and since June 1994 I have chaired the board. The work we accomplish in Promise Keepers to heal racial barriers strikes a chord in my heart. Through firsthand experience I've learned about racial walls and how they can be taken down.

One of my sons, Arthur, attended graduate school

in Atlanta, Georgia. Atlanta is very different from Denver, particularly in the strong push toward cultural identity. After Arthur saw that, he came home and told me, "Daddy, you don't know what it means to be black anymore. You've lived in this white world so long that you don't understand the hurts and pains anymore. Black people went through some hard stuff."

I was shocked. Why did Arthur think my life was smooth sailing? Then it hit me like a ton of bricks — I had never told Arthur about the pain of the past. I didn't want to bring up things that were negative. I wanted his foundation to be positive.

While I've worked for many years for reconciliation, during my growing up years I didn't dwell on the prejudice in our society. Instead I saw closed doors as opportunities for the Holy Spirit to work in my life.

That day I resolved that Arthur would know what forces created Phillip H. Porter, Jr.

RECRUITED TO BREAK DOWN THE WALLS AT PHILLIPS

When I was in high school in 1954 I was recruited by Lincoln University in Jefferson City, Missouri. They offered me a dual scholarship — for football and for my academic credentials. I was also a successful boxer at the time. Then during the third game of my senior year in high school I broke three vertebrae, and my football days were over. Yet Lincoln still offered me the academic scholarship.

A Supreme Court decision in 1954 changed my college plans. In the case of *Brown v. Topeka Board of Education,* the court declared that the separate-but-equal doctrine was wrong. As a result schools had to integrate.

I was ecstatic about the ruling. Little did I know that I would be personally asked to play a role in this historic event.

Phillips University, an all-white school in my hometown of Enid, Oklahoma, was on a search for black students to integrate their school. This university, which was associated with the Disciples of Christ denomination, called my local black high school to see if any students qualified to attend. My principal, Luther W. Elliott, Sr., thought about me and said, "I know just the guy for you — Phillip Porter."

Along with Professor Elliott I went to meet the president of the university, Dr. Eugene S. Briggs. We sat in the high-back, deep-red leather chairs of his office and talked. Dr. Briggs had read about my success as a Golden Gloves boxer and had seen my academic qualifications. Dr. Briggs offered me a $250 scholarship — the total amount for four years.

"We've also arranged some social life for you at Phillips," he said with a smile. "We've recruited a black girl named Lois Mothershed from Little Rock for next year's class. Lois sings like an angel, and she's from the Disciples church." Some social life! His conversation implied that Lois was my only possibility for social life among the other college students.

"There's one more thing, Phillip," Dr. Briggs said. "Integration will not be without problems. We've never had black students studying in close proximity to white students. This is a Christian college, and we're trying to integrate peacefully. We know about your successful fights in boxing, and I want you to promise that you will not fight." I assured Dr. Briggs that my boxing and fighting days were over.

"You'll have to take a lot of flack from people, Phillip," Dr. Briggs continued. "Can you do it?"

"I can keep calm in any situation," I reassured the president.

WATERMELON ON MY FACE

On the first day of orientation for the school a large group of students met on the school baseball field. The school set up tables with watermelon, and on that August day we enjoyed the fresh fruit. I walked along carrying my piece of melon and smiling at people. I'd stop and introduce myself to people making light conversation. It was my desire to fit into my new school.

Suddenly a big red-headed boy from Louisiana rushed over and slammed my face into the melon I was carrying. He laughed and said, "I always wanted to put a nigger's face in a melon."

I forgot my promise to Dr. Briggs, and with fury I turned loose my boxing skills on this rude kid and whipped him. A few minutes later both of us were standing in Dr. Briggs office.

The president shook his head in disappointment. "Phillip, I told you it would be difficult. You promised me that you wouldn't fight, and here you are fighting before classes even start." I apologized for letting him down.

Because the red-haired student initiated the fight, he was immediately suspended from the school and

23

sent back home to Louisiana. After the boy left the room Dr. Briggs turned to me. "You need to keep yourself under control, Phillip," he cautioned. "You may face things worse than this during your four years at Phillips University." I consciously made an effort to keep my emotions under control. I thought to myself, *I'm here. I've been chosen by God, by my parents, by my community, by this school, to help integrate. My job is to do that. I've got to help integrate.*

I repeated those words to myself during the remainder of my college years. But I held myself under control and wasn't drawn into another fight. Sure there were opportunities, but I resisted the temptation to lash back with my fists.

I was foolhardy enough to pledge an all-white social services club. This club was like a fraternity or sorority. During pledge week we were blind-folded at about 2 A.M. and taken into the country. The older members let us out on the side of the road, and we had to find our way back to the university. Two of us — a black and a white — entered a farm yard and the farmer almost shot us.

I had several abrasive times. People called me "nigger." When I played intramural sports, some-times the white students would team up against me. But I accepted every incident as a part of integrating the university.

A principle I learned and practiced was to blend into the school. I constantly tried to meet new people and get to know them. The students gave an annual award for class friendliness to one male and one female student. During my freshman and sophomore years I was voted the class friendliest by my fellow students. During my junior year I received the award of all-school friendliest male.

I had learned a value from my black high school — one which came out of our schools being segregated. The teachers constantly told us, "If you want to make it in this world, you have to be twice as good as the white folk. You've got to work harder and longer. You've got to be more polite and be more intense — twice as good."

The scholarship didn't go very far toward covering my expenses. When I graduated at the end of my four years, I owed the school several thousand dollars in bills, even though I worked forty hours a week. There was no provision from the school for room or board. I lived at home, and during the first semester I drove to school in my little car. In the bitter, cold winter the engine in my car froze and broke. Now without a vehicle, I continued to try and maintain my appearance of having a car. Every day I got up early and walked the ten miles from home to school to attend my classes which sometimes started at 7 A.M.

After classes I went to work. Every day I said goodbye to my friends and walked toward the parking lot. I was so full of pride that I didn't want anyone to know I didn't have a car. Once I got far enough I would slip out the other side of the lot. There was no bus service to the restaurant where I worked, so again I walked another seven or eight miles. Each day I worked as a fry cook from 4 P.M. until midnight. With a forty-hour work week and a full load of classes, I was determined to be "twice as good as the white folk." I worked hard to maintain my facade at Phillips.

There is a caution with blending into your environment and working at racial reconciliation. Sometimes you can carry it too far, and I learned about this while at Phillips on the speech squad. We traveled to different universities and competed against their schools. Often on these trips I had to sleep and eat in another place than the rest of the team. As the only black member, the races were often kept separate. But on one trip to Kansas I was housed with the white students.

In my subconscious I forgot who I was and became white. In the morning as I was eating breakfast I glanced in a nearby mirror and saw the reflection of a black hand. I quickly pulled my hand away from the view of the mirror. *Whose black hand is that?* I thought. It was a turning point for me because I realized that black hand was mine. Sometimes I was ashamed of my blackness. While at Phillips on that speech squad, I felt that I had made it in the white man's world — but I had carried my experience too far.

I felt broken and hurt. As a student of sociology I had learned an important lesson about prejudice and the movement of racial reconciliation. When there is only one person, a black among whites or a white among blacks, there is a tendency to forget who you are and where you've come from.

I include this story as a caution in our journey toward racial reconciliation. In terms of nutrition, it takes different food groups to make a complete meal. For example, the vegetable group must be present to make the bread group unique. The same is true with reconciliation. We need each other to be distinct racial groups within the human race. Blacks must be present to make the whites unique and vice versa.

I see people struggle with this in the African American congregation I pastor at All Nations Pentecostal Center Church of God in Christ. A number of whites who are married to blacks have tried to become black in their mannerisms. These people have even changed hairstyles to look like blacks. They failed to appreciate the beauty of diversity. The red rose is beautiful but so are the white and yellow roses.

That morning in Kansas I got up from the table and didn't eat my breakfast. I had blended in so well that I gave up my identity. I had thought, *We're all white folks here together on this speech squad.* But I wasn't white. I had just lost my blackness.

For racial reconciliation to occur in our world, it will take more than one person. One person is too likely to be swallowed up by the larger group. Two people are better and three or more are much better. Great numbers of people need to be working on this important area of our society. Instead of bowing to the pressure to blend into society, we need to celebrate who we are in Christ.

My First "Job" Out of College

Before my junior year in college I began courting the beautiful Edgar Lee Moye. She and her family were members of the church my father pastored.

We were married after a nine-month courtship, and a few months into our marriage Lee became pregnant with our first child, Phillip. Then, shortly before graduation, the Lord blessed us with our second child, Catherine.

Lois Mothershed and I were the first two African American graduates from Phillips in 1959. With a bachelor of arts degree in sociology and with a recommendation from my major sociology professor, I found a job in social work in the southern Colorado town of Walsenburg. After a phone interview their office sent me a letter which confirmed my job and the time and place for my arrival.

Leaving my wife and two children temporarily in Oklahoma, I got on a bus and traveled to Walsenburg. Although my first day wasn't until Monday, I arrived the Thursday before to go into the office and meet my coworkers. I entered the office and introduced myself, "Hello, I'm Phillip Porter, and I'm here for the job."

My presence caused a stir among the workers in the office, but I didn't make much of it. The supervisor came to the front of the office and told me, "I'm sorry but that job has been filled." That didn't put me off because I knew that I was the one who had filled the job.

"Yes," I said, "I'm the one who has filled the job. In fact, I've got the letter here to prove it." I reached in my suit coat and pulled out my letter from the supervisor. It gave details like my job description, time to report for my orientation and the name of the supervisor.

"No, the job has been filled," the supervisor said

as he reached across and snatched my letter from my hands. As I watched in horror, he tore the letter into small pieces and dropped it into the trash can. "There is no position here." Evidently, the office had expected me to be a white student from an all-white school. I lost the job because I was black.

In shock I turned and walked out of the office. I was hurt, first of all. And astonished. I felt defenseless. My baser nature wanted to reach across the counter and punch that guy out for good. What would I do now? I had no plan B. A great number of people in my hometown of Enid had sent me off with excitement. What in the world would I tell them? My wife and kids were counting on this job, and now the door had slammed shut.

At this moment I had to decide what this experience would do to me. I could become angry and bitter and take out my vengeance for the rest of my life. Instead, I decided to go on with the faith that God had orchestrated my education and that He had orchestrated my being in Walsenburg. I had to believe in the goodness of God and the justice of God to work out His purpose for my life. This was a temporary setback.

My duty was to seek Him as it says in Jeremiah 29:13, "And you will seek Me and find Me, when you search for Me with all your heart." This search must occur in all areas: intellectual, physical, spiritual, emotional.

For me the first step was a change in physical location. I got on a bus and began the four-hour ride to Denver where my brother-in-law lived, wondering all the while what God held in store for my future.

POINTS TO PONDER

1. Think about the walls in your own life. Pinpoint one area where you'd like to break down these walls. Maybe it's race. Maybe it's across denominations. Maybe it is in your marriage or with a family member.

   ✓ Have you ever lost something that you fully expected to receive? Maybe you lost a job that you had accepted, or a relationship which you thought would last forever.

   ✓ How did you handle the rejection?

2. In this chapter you read about how I handled the rejection of my social work position. You also saw how initially I rejected Coach Bill McCartney and the men from Promise Keepers when they came to my church.

   ✓ From these personal stories, what principles can you draw for your own life and relationships?

   ✓ Is rejection a cause for bitterness and regret, or do you see these situations as opportunities for the Holy Spirit to open other doors in your life?

3. Sometimes prejudice rears its ugly head in a forthright way — like when I was

rejected outright for that social work position because of my race. But other times prejudice subtly slips into our lives. Think about how I assumed Coach Mac committed an act of prejudice against one of his players. Yet when I confronted him I realized prejudice had slipped into my own judgment.

✓ How prominent is prejudice in your own life and relationships?

4. The apostle Paul admonishes Timothy in 1 Timothy 5:21 in regard to a number of relationship questions.

✓ Read 1 Timothy 5:21 and think of ways you can avoid prejudice in your relationships.

CHAPTER 2

FROM THE CLAY
OF OKLAHOMA

've always had a desire to break down the walls within my African American race as well as between African Americans and other racial groups. My bus ride from Walsenburg (the place where I thought I had a job) to Denver shows my involvement in this area.

When I got on the bus, I noticed another young African American man sitting in the back, which was the usual place we sat in those days.

I nodded at the well-dressed and quite somber

young man. He didn't return my nod, but gave me a look which said, "Don't bother me."

What does that fellow mean giving me a look which says, "Leave me alone?" We were the only two blacks on this four-hour bus ride to Denver. *There must be some common ground that we can find for a relationship.*

His response made me feel uneasy, but I was not easily put off. I chose a seat some distance in front of him and sat down. For a while I sat still. Then, when I couldn't contain myself any longer, I got up and moved farther back in the bus. I took the seat beside him, and I pressed along into a conversation.

I introduced myself saying, "I'm Phillip Porter. What's your name?"

"I'm Richard Morris," he finally said with a reluctant tone.

"I'm a college graduate going to Denver and looking for work," I said to continue the conversation, and I noticed he was beginning to look more relaxed as the scenery raced past us.

"I'm a college student as well from Southern University in Baton Rouge, Louisiana."

"Are you saved?" I asked.

"Oh, yes. I'm a minister, and I'm starting to preach," he said.

From the way he answered, I knew immediately Richard was a part of the Church of God in Christ. During this time and in this part of the country we were the only ones to describe ourselves as being saved.

"Church of God in Christ?" I asked.

"Why, how did you know?" he exclaimed.

We found common ground for conversation. Before long we reached into our wallets and showed our family pictures. When I pointed out a photo of my sister Shirley, who was two years younger, this reserved, quiet young man suddenly sat up alert and attentive. "Is she married?" he asked.

"No," I said.

"Do you mind if I get her address and write her?" Richard said.

I chuckled at the changes in the man's demeanor. "I'd be happy to give you her address."

Our conversation continued until we reached the Denver bus station. A week later by pure coincidence Richard Morris and I attended the same church. He began to write my sister. In the meantime my wife and children had moved to Denver, and eventually Shirley asked if she could move from Oklahoma to live with us. Richard and Shirley dated, and in December 1959 they were married. More than thirty-five years later they are still married. It began with my reaching out and befriending a man in the back of a bus. I valued this young man as a person. This attitude is a key principle in the work of reconciliation.

WHAT NEXT?

When I arrived in Denver I wondered, *What next?* I considered my skills. Throughout high school and college I had worked as a fry cook in a restaurant. I began in the restaurant business at age twelve by washing dishes. I worked my way through the next nine years by cooking, butchering and baking.

As I paged through the classified ads in the *Denver Post* I found a position at a restaurant called The White Spot located at the corner of Eighth and Broadway. This job was the only one in the newspaper that jumped out at me.

"Do you know how to cook?" the owner asked me. I felt a bit indignant that he even asked me such a question. During my interview I had presented myself as a college graduate from Phillips University in Oklahoma.

I replied, *"Anything* you've got in this place, I can cook." He hired me for the position. As my new employer got to know me he gave me more and more responsibility. Before long I was the manager of the night shift for The White Spot. When the door for my job in Walsenburg slammed shut the Holy Spirit opened another door for me in Denver.

While working at The White Spot I put into practice a key principle of tearing down the walls and moving toward reconciliation. I learned to increase my sensitivity to relationships. I don't mean that I became so sensitive that I simply fell apart at any confrontation. Instead I became aware of prejudice or discrimination when it crossed my path, so I plotted a strategy for change.

At The White Spot we used buckets from Kentucky Fried Chicken for our take-out orders. Printed on the side of every bucket were the words from the state song for Kentucky, "My Old Kentucky Home," by Stephen Foster. Part of the lyrics say, "In the summer the darkies are gay." I found the phrase offensive and didn't want to serve chicken in those buckets. I waited for an appropriate moment and registered my complaint with the owners of the restaurant.

They quickly said, "Hey, we just buy these buckets from Kentucky Fried Chicken. They are a national franchise, and we can't do anything about it." But after their initial protests they proposed an idea which held the possibility for change. "Next week Colonel Sanders is going to be in Denver for a few days. Why don't you talk with him about these offensive lyrics? He has the ability to remove these words."

A few days later I met with Colonel Sanders. The old gentleman patiently listened to my complaint about the lyrics on his buckets of chicken. He understood my concern, but no matter how much I pressed him the Colonel wouldn't commit to changing anything. I liked the fact that he wasn't defensive but listened as I made my case for change. I walked away from the meeting with no promises, yet I had a calm assurance that something would change. A few months later we got new buckets from Kentucky Fried Chicken for The White Spot. The offensive lyrics had disappeared. The new buckets were plain.

AMBASSADOR TO THE NEIGHBORHOOD

As I worked at The White Spot, I sometimes spent long hours alone. It gave me time to reflect on the journey that brought me from a small town in Oklahoma to Denver. Yet I knew the journey would not end in restaurant work.

My parents told me that even while I was in my mother's womb, they prayed I would be a boy and that I would preach. I was born at 11:37 A.M. on a

Sunday morning and entered the world squalling. My parents said, "Yeah, that's a good sign that Phillip will be a preacher."

Throughout my early years my parents nurtured me and helped me feel that I was special. When I was about four years old my dad, an itinerant preacher, got a piece of land in Enid, Oklahoma, to build a three-room house for our family on. Our lot was located right on the border between the black and the white communities. Across the street from our house was a large, white elementary school.

Every morning I would dress like I was headed to kindergarten, but I didn't go anywhere because I wasn't old enough for school. I'd comb my hair and put on my best clothing. Then I'd walk out to the front of our house and stand on the side of the road. I'd wave to everyone who came past the house. It was as though I held the position of "Ambassador to the Neighborhood" for blacks and whites. People told my parents, "That boy gives us inspiration."

As a small child I felt that greeting folks who went past my house was a part of my calling. I gained an appreciation and friendliness toward people. Even today I greet people with a smile and a nod as I enter a restaurant or walk down the street. Those early days of waving to people has helped shape my lifelong journey as a reconciler who tears down the walls between people.

Across the street from our house was a white family with children about our ages. Those white children always crossed the street and came to our house. While we never thought about the distinction, we were never invited to their house nor were we invited to play with their white friends.

Usually we played "house." I'd be the daddy and the little white girl would be the mommy. I pretended to go to work. Then I came home and read the newspaper. She would play like she was cooking up a little something, and then we would play eating together. From these early friendships, I was raised with a propensity to reach out to people — no matter what their race or color.

SELF-WORTH AND THE TIME NOT TO SHOW IT

When I was nine I worked with my grandfather on a trash truck. At that time the city didn't haul trash, so enterprising individuals started their own businesses to collect garbage. We picked up trash in wealthy communities and downtown. I remember on those routes we had to use restrooms that were marked "colored" or water fountains labeled "colored."

When I was about twelve our trash route included an oil refinery. One day a large, jovial man who was behind a desk called out to me, "How are you doing, smokie?" The term *smokie* was derogatory like *blackie* or *nigger*, so I simply ignored his question.

"Do you hear me, smokie boy?" the man tried again. "How are you doing, smokie?"

My parents made me feel proud of my name so I turned and said, "If you're talking to me, my name isn't smokie. My name is Phillip."

"What are you saying, boy?" his tone had changed from jovial to serious.

My grandfather was within earshot and heard the entire exchange. He jumped into the conversation. "He didn't say nothing. He didn't say nothing." Then my grandfather laughed nervously and said, "We're going now. Goodbye."

A few minutes later Grandfather ushered me into his truck, and we roared down the road. He said, "Don't you *ever* do that again to a white man. He will get you and get me and lynch us."

"You mean he can call me smokie and I can't tell him no?" I asked. I thought to myself, *I can't be treated so unfairly and improperly. Things have to change.*

A Sense of Humor

When I was growing up I admired my dad's tremendous sense of humor. He was born in 1899, the son of a pastor. He lived in Darby, Pennsylvania, where my grandfather helped build the First Baptist Church of Darby that still bears his name in the cornerstone.

Dad appeared a shade darker than I am. Dad jokingly called the boys in our family "black boys." He changed the derogatory terms of the day for African Americans into a joke or something to laugh about. His humor and attitude affirmed our self-worth. Sometimes in the front yards of white people we'd see little figurines of blacks. My dad pointed them out and laughed. It helped us maintain our sense of humor about the temperament of the times.

OUTFOX THE BULLIES

Throughout grade school my good study habits created jealousy among some of my classmates. For weeks they tried to corner me after school and beat me up. When this failed they chased me, and their efforts increased in intensity. But they could not manage to catch me. I had built a network of friends on the path from school to my home. Merchants and friends would hide me until the bullies passed.

Once I convinced the other kids in my neighborhood that the bullies were chasing poor kids. We set up a plan to get back at them at a certain intersection. "When I turn the corner tomorrow you be ready for them," I said. My friends collected sticks, bricks and tin cans. It was a great game plan.

The day was like any other. As always I ran down the block and tore around the corner. Then my friends poured out of their houses, screaming and unleashing their ammunition on our shared enemy. The gang turned and ran away. Through working together we had a neighborhood victory, but my celebration was short-lived.

The next day the same group blocked my path home, and I couldn't get around them. But they didn't know I had also built relationships with the merchants in the white section of town. So instead of running south toward home I ran west into the white area of the city.

I ran into a little grocery store and cried out to the owners, "Some guys in a gang are chasing me and want to beat me up. Can you help me?"

"Crouch down here quickly behind the counter,"

the man said as the gang entered the store. They spotted me behind the counter and couldn't believe it. They asked, "Does he work here?"

The woman said, "Yeah, he works for us, and if you bother him anymore then I'm going to let your parents know about it." The guys walked out of the store and stood outside trying to decide what to do next. I ducked out the side door, and I ran past them to my home.

From these incidents I learned how to use my mind for confrontation. The lessons from these situations helped me in the days ahead with working for racial reconciliation. But I didn't always escape.

One day three guys caught me and cornered me on the way home. They began to punch me, and I said, "Hey somebody's going to get hurt if you don't be careful."

"Oh, yeah, you're the one who is going to get hurt," one of them growled. In panic I swung and connected with the biggest guy's chin. I was trying to connect with anyone. To my surprise he fell to the ground. The guys looked at their friend and said, "Get up, Ballard." They crouched down over their friend for a closer look. He was clearly knocked out. The fight was over. The word got around that I had knocked out this tough guy and that I was the new bully.

For the next few weeks I had people lined up to fight with me after school. An older friend who lived near my home was a boxer. One day he said to me, "Phillip, unless you go to the gym and learn how to fight, these guys are going to kill you. Why don't you let me teach you?"

I went into the boxing gym and learned how to fight. Eventually I became a Golden Gloves boxer in the welterweight category. I learned how to defend myself and fight in an organized system rather than just on the street. As a championship fighter I fought fifty-three times and won forty-nine of those events. In fact, I went semipro in my circles of boxing.

During this period of my life I traveled with my dad to Royce City, Texas, which was near Dallas. We were going to see my older sister who was married. On our return trip we took our car into the service station to have it serviced. In many ways, I had forgotten about the segregation between blacks and whites. I walked over to a drinking fountain at the service station. The white man checking under the hood of our car straightened up and shouted across to me, "Hey, boy, don't drink that water."

I looked puzzled and said, "What?"

"Don't drink that water, boy! Hey, nigger, did you hear me? Don't drink that water!"

I came unglued. With my fighting experience I was ready to take this guy apart. I said, "What? I'll drink it if I want to. You make me tired."

My dad came up and said, "Sir, I'm sorry. He didn't mean that. He's sorry." And my dad moved me away from the confrontation. We got in the car and drove away from the station.

I fumed at my dad, "Dad, I'm not a kid anymore. I wanted to whip this guy. I don't have to take junk like that."

Dad replied, "You're going to take it this time. We're both here alone, and these folks down here will wear us out." Dad knew those people could beat us or hang us or whatever they wanted to do. It was not the time nor place to fight back over a drink of water. This taught me there is wisdom in selecting which situations are worth a fight.

FAIR TREATMENT — WHEN LASHING BACK BACKFIRES

As we work through the concept of prejudice in our society and our relationships, one battle cry is often heard, "That's not fair." How do we find fair treatment in an unfair and unbalanced world? Once I took matters of fairness into my own hands, and it completely backfired on me.

When I was fifteen my father had problems with ulcers and was hospitalized in Oklahoma City. Because I was the oldest son I had to pick up my dad's janitorial work in Enid. He cleaned a variety of places, but one of his consistent jobs was a local tavern.

Each day I emptied trash, swept, mopped the floors, cleaned spittoons and stacked cases of beer. It took my two younger brothers and I several hours to finish the work. At the end of the week the owner paid me. I was shocked at the amount — fifteen dollars for seven days of hard work. I looked angrily at the money and said, "Fifteen dollars?" "Oh, yeah, and here's the leftover candy," the man said as he reached behind the counter and dumped some old bars of candy into a small bag. "Don't you remember that your dad brought home candy?" I didn't say anything else, but inside I felt burned and angry about this whole line of thinking. To this man the leftover candy took the place of proper payment for our work.

In the 1950s such treatment was commonplace, and as a black person I didn't dare get too smart-alecky. I accepted the payment from the man, but in my heart I had a desire to get back at him and receive what was rightly ours.

After that I took a little money from the cash register everyday. Not any amount that would be noticed but just a few quarters and dimes. One morning after we were finished with our cleaning I reached into the cash register and took some money as I usually did. Suddenly the manager emerged from behind several boxes. Since our arrival he had been hiding just waiting for something like this to happen. He caught me red-handed with my hand in his cash register.

"Caught you!" he yelled as he sprang into the room.

I backed up with my hands up in the air and a horrified look on my face. I still had his money in my hands.

"I knew I was missing some money from that register! Why I ought to throw you into jail for stealing from me, but it was only a few missing quarters," he sputtered with his face turning red.

"Instead of throwing you into jail, I'm going to do the next best thing," he threatened. "I'm going to take you home, tell your mother, then fire you."

He carried through with his plans. My mother was disappointed but eventually forgave me.

My attempt at fair treatment through stealing coins backfired, but it taught me an unforgettable lesson. Sometimes we feel like fighting back. We feel like stealing what we believe the world ought to offer us. But if we take these actions to try to right the prejudice of the world and society, it doesn't change things.

I learned to turn these feelings over to God and to look at the bigger picture of my life and where I was headed. My parents knew that stealing doesn't change the world. It only heaps on more guilt. My dad knew the reality of Proverbs 30:7-9, "Two things I request of You (Deprive me not before I die): Remove falsehood and lies far from me; Give me neither poverty nor riches — Feed me with the food You allotted to me; Lest I be full and deny You, and say, 'Who is the Lord?' Or lest I be poor and steal, and profane the name of my God." I didn't want to dishonor the Lord, and stealing was no way to get ahead.

My parents wanted me to be the first to complete college then get a good job. Through education and living for God they believed I could make a difference in my world and overcome these feelings of prejudice. Also if I had a college degree I could secure a better job, and stealing would be unnecessary. But I couldn't get an education if I got in trouble stealing. My one-time experience taught me a hard but important lesson, and I'll never forget it.

After I was caught stealing we lost fifteen dollars per week, and it was hard on our family. I felt responsible to earn money for our family — especially during my dad's illness and recovery. Where could I earn more money?

The military. I looked older than my sixteen years, so I exaggerated my age and tried to join the service. During this time the Korean War was raging. I could go off to Korea, fight for my country and send home most of my earnings from the military. It would delay my going to college, but my family needed the money.

I went downtown to the recruiting office and picked up the paperwork. I had one more hurdle to cross before I could join — Mama.

When I showed Mama the papers, she refused to sign them. "Even if I have to work, Phillip, I will see that you go to college," she said with a determined look on her face. The discussion was ended. I was headed toward a college.

I felt such great love from my parents. They strengthened my belief in my self-worth. Likewise in our journeys of reconciliation we'll need the support of parents, spouses or special brothers and sisters in Christ. These loved ones will believe in us when our self-confidence may wane or waiver. Proverbs 17:17 says, "A friend loves at all times, and a brother is born for adversity." The confidence of our friends and loved ones can sustain us along the sometimes bumpy and difficult path against prejudice.

With the support of my parents I went back to my high school studies with an even greater determination to follow the Lord and get a quality education. I knew that every step of the journey my parents would continue to be supportive and encouraging.

THE FIRST SIT-IN

While I was in high school I joined three young men and a young woman to create a black newspaper for our region. The five of us had many idealistic ideas. Before sit-ins became popular we decided it would be nice to have the privilege of joining other people for a refreshing soda and an ice cream at the popular drugstore in the town square. As a group we were committed to sitting at their counter until we were served. We selected a Saturday morning in 1954 when we didn't have school and could sit all day if necessary.

In those days much of Enid's activities were conducted in or around the town square. The center of town was the location for the county court house, the jail and the only decent public restrooms, both white and colored. The post office was there, and many people picked up their mail since there was little home delivery. Plus department store shopping was available.

Into this scene we entered the Stunkle Rexall Drug Store at 9 A.M. that Saturday morning. We sat at the soda fountain. "The counter isn't open yet," one of the employees told us.

"That's OK. We can wait," we politely responded. We were on a mission to tear down this wall of segregation. At about noon they tried to get us to leave the counter saying, "You'll need to leave now because this area will be used by the people for whom it is intended."

We smiled and were polite but firm, "We will be staying until we are served." Of course all of us were not of the same temperament. But I was the spokesperson, and I was careful that we didn't antagonize anyone. We accomplished this low-key protest by continuing conversation and behaving in a very polite manner. The owner of the drugstore didn't want any publicity and attempted to keep the scene cordial.

However, by about 1 P.M. newspaper reporters showed up with cameras, note pads and pencils. The crowd grew larger, but there were never any unruly situations.

At about 4 P.M. the owner ordered his employees to serve us. With great jubilation we ate our sandwiches and drank sodas, then paid for them, thanked people and left. There were cheers, and a few jeers, and several of us gave comments to the reporters. We felt a sense of victory not only for ourselves, but for our city. While such protests were going on across the nation, we were not sophisticated enough to think in terms of a national movement. We were simply pleased that we had protested and won. In 1960 a similar sit-in by four students at a lunch counter in Greensboro, North Carolina, would begin desegregation in the South and become a national rallying point for the civil rights movement.

The real victory from our protest, in my perspective, came in 1994 during a chance meeting I had with the original owner's son. I had traveled back to Enid for a visit and decided to drop by the drugstore as an old site of remembrance. As I went into the drugstore, which remained in the same location, I introduced myself and inquired about the original owner. The clerk informed me that the new manager/owner would like to see me.

I brought up the incident from 1954 with him and to my great surprise he said, "Yes, that was my father who passed away only last year." Then he added, "I was in the Navy at that time, and my dad sent me the clipping about the incident. I always wondered about what happened to those students." We shook hands and smiled at the memory that had brought us together. Then we had a soda and thanked God that era had passed.

Looking back I realized how much I had learned about tearing down racial walls, and sometimes a high price was paid for doing it.

POINTS TO PONDER

1. I could have chosen to ignore the "don't bother me" look from the other person in the back of the bus on my ride to Denver. I was brought to a point of making a decision, and I decided to pursue a relationship.

    Choices, small and large, fill our lives every day. It's important to consider how we make these choices because they influence whether we will be people who move toward healing or people who continue the hurt of prejudice in our world. The person who wants to move toward healing will reach out to others. This requires risking rejection; it means increasing sensitivity to the needs of others. The opposite response is to build a wall around your life and live without connection to other people.

    ✓ Evaluate the interaction with others you had today. Were there situations in which you hid behind your wall and others in which you reached out with a kind word or action?

    ✓ What steps can you take to increase these kind and reconciling actions?

    ✓ As I interacted with Richard Morris on the four-hour bus trip, I valued him as another person. Consider your relationships with other people — coworkers, family or friends. How are you telling them that you value your relationship with them? Through your words? Through your notes of encouragement? Through your actions?

✔ Talk about your past actions and your goals for the future with a friend, and ask him to check back with you on your progress.

2. "What next?" I asked myself when a door of opportunity was slammed shut in my field of social work.

✔ Have you had a door slammed in your face because of a wall of race, prejudice, denominationalism or another relational conflict?

✔ How do you handle these situations?

At such a point of decision you can let bitterness and regret fill your life. The Bible guarantees that such a course will be filled with misery (Heb. 12:14-15). Or you can follow the example from my life and look for God to open another door of opportunity.

3. As you look for this opportunity, evaluate your skills and possibilities. I knew immediately that I could work as a fry cook, so I stepped out and took the position. The

well-known Bible teacher Paul Little wrote, "God can't steer a parked car." We need to be on the move for God to use our lives in the movement of reconciliation, tearing down the relational walls in our lives.

4. "I'll try it." Sometimes that simple statement of willingness will make a difference. For example, when the words on the side of the Kentucky Fried Chicken buckets bothered me, I could have ignored them. Instead I chose to make an appointment and talk with Colonel Sanders. When we see the walls of prejudice, we can choose to let them remain or take steps to remove the walls.

✓ What walls do you face in your own life and situation?

✓ How can you take some steps of action to break down the walls?

5. Several places in this chapter, I tell about name-calling, which serves to build walls between us. You might not be using derogatory racist words, but you might be thinking that someone else is dumb, slow or stupid.

✓ How is name-calling active in your own life?

✓ Be honest with yourself and your relationships. What steps can you take to stop name-calling?

6. While sometimes we stand and fight in the midst of confrontation, other times there is wisdom in running away. In our work for reconciliation, often we need to exercise wisdom. Reflect on a time when you were faced with possible confrontation but you exercised wisdom and moved away from confrontation.

7. My story about unfairness indicates another aspect of reconciliation. We can't act against the law or take matters into our own hands — such as my stealing from the cash register.

   ✓ Have you ever tried to go against the law and take matters of unfairness into your own hands?

   ✓ What have the positive results been? The negative results?

   ✓ How can we turn these feelings of unfairness over to God and ask God's justice to prevail in our lives?

   Take a few moments and commit these situations into God's hands and ask for His justice and His wisdom.

8. What is one thing you can do to make a difference (like my story of the drugstore sit-in)?

   ✓ Are you committed to making a difference?

✓ What if it involves publicity? What if
there is no publicity? Does this
bother you?

✓ Have you returned to any past situation and discovered the results of your
prior actions?

✓ How can you address some of the
injustices that come to your attention?

CHAPTER 3

THE PRICE OF TEARING DOWN THE WALLS

The little white church looked like it belonged on the cover of a church bulletin. It was picture-perfect with a small picket fence around part of its yard and a bell on a steeple. The building was on a corner lot just off Highway 64, and it was located in a small town west of Enid, Oklahoma. Each of these towns had a reputation for being fiercely prejudiced and diligent about enforcing segregation policies, but that didn't stop us from going there.

It was 1953, and at sixteen years of age I traveled to this church with two white women from the Women's Christian Temperance Union (WCTU). The WCTU fought gallantly against the evils of alcohol and tobacco. They were also committed to promoting peace among races. The organization ran essay contests, and I often spoke at these gatherings. I spoke to civic groups like Kiwanis, Rotary and Lions Clubs throughout this region in Oklahoma. But this day was different.

It was Reconciliation Sunday. The congregation of the little white church had invited the WCTU to provide a speaker. I was the choice of these women but not the choice of the congregation. When I walked into the meeting, I noticed that some people turned red-faced at my arrival. Looking around the room at other people, I could see how they were turned off by me. They were present at the meeting physically but not with their attention. During the opening prayers and songs I sat on the platform and looked over the audience. Then the leader of the WCTU introduced me as the speaker, and I walked to the podium.

As I positioned my notes and began to speak, two men stood up. With great stir, these two men moved to the side of the small sanctuary. They were protesting that a colored person was speaking at their church. Silently one of the men motioned to the WCTU leader. She walked to the back of the building and talked with the men.

"Yes," she whispered to the man. "What can I do for you?"

"That nigger," one of the men whispered in her

ear and gestured over in my direction. "Why did you bring him? You need to cut him short. We don't want to listen to him speak on reconciliation. We find it offensive."

"Phillip Porter is our choice for today's speaker," the woman calmly said. "I will not stop him from speaking."

"We'll see about that," the man gruffed. She returned to her seat. I didn't let the commotion deter me from my speech, but I knew that something was going to happen. Inside I knew it had something to do with me. My black face in the midst of an all-white congregation had made an impression. Even so, I didn't worry about it because such a setting was fairly typical for my other WCTU speeches.

Although I don't remember many specifics from my message, I know that during my sermon I told a story from my childhood.

When I was a young boy growing up in Oklahoma, Sunday morning church services in our town were a segregated hour. Blacks went to their own church and had their own style of worship, while white people attended their services. Everywhere I went I could see signs of segregation. But on Sunday evenings something different happened.

At our small Church of God in Christ church my family gathered with other people for a worship service. When I was only about four years old, I remember that the congregation had a mixture of races — white people sat beside black people; Native Americans sat beside white people. Our focus wasn't on where we sat but who we came to worship. Through our music we lifted the One who transcended any race and creed — the Lord Jesus Christ.

During church the color of the people in attendance didn't make any difference. From all over the congregation people spoke an "amen" or "That's right, brother." When the pastor gave the invitation, once again race wasn't an issue. Whites, blacks, Native Americans and even a few Hispanics walked to the front of the church and knelt at the altar. Everyone needed a touch from God in their lives — for healing, for salvation and for strength to make it through the week ahead.

From these experiences as a young black in Oklahoma, I knew that the walls of segregation could be broken and that Jesus Christ could transform people so they forgot about race. Now as I spoke to this all-white congregation, reconciliation was the theme of my message. I painted a picture of equality in God's kingdom and equal opportunity for all people — no matter which race they are or which background they come from. In the eyes of the almighty God, the field was perfectly level.

Yet as I spoke to the small crowd of white people, I could see the agitation and disbelief on their faces. The two men were still looking for a way to stop my message.

Out of the corner of my eye I saw them motion to their pastor. Reluctantly the elderly man rose from his seat and walked to the back of the room.

"Get that nigger off the platform, or you'll be looking for a new church," the man threatened his pastor.

This parishioner had a great deal of influence in

the church, and the pastor knew the reality of this threat. He motioned for the WCTU leader and explained the situation. A few minutes later she handed me a note. While speaking I opened it and read, "Finish your talk in three minutes." I quickly concluded my message.

As I left the church, people were distantly polite with their conversation and handshakes. Some of their faces burned with anger. They were probably thinking, *The very idea of this colored boy coming to our nice, little, white church on Sunday and talking about reconciliation.*

After the service the women took me home. In the car, with tears in their eyes and regret in their voices, they explained why my speech had been cut short. "It wasn't you, Phillip," one of the women said. "You did a good job, but we're living in difficult times. People aren't ready to listen to what you have to say." In terms of breaking down the walls of prejudice these two women from the WCTU were ahead of their time.

On another occasion they took me to a different town. My message turned into a discussion with the audience. One man interrupted me angrily and said, "We don't have any Negroes in this town, so how do you think we can be friends with them? The only people of race that we have in this area are a few Mexican Americans and some Native Americans. And all the Indians want to do is to scalp us." When I left that small town in Oklahoma, I knew that the wall of prejudice was firmly in place.

For more than forty years I've been speaking on reconciliation, and although some walls have been broken down it is evident this is as much an individual struggle as it is a collective effort. The reality and truth of 2 Corinthians 5:17-18 needs to break through and change our lives. That passage of Scripture says:

> Therefore, if anyone is in Christ, he is a new creation; old things have passed away; behold, all things have become new. Now all things are of God, who has reconciled us to Himself through Jesus Christ, and has given us the *ministry of reconciliation* (italics added).

It was in Christ that God was reconciling the world to Himself. And because we are in Christ, God has committed to us the ministry of breaking down the walls.

As a teenager I spoke often about reconciliation and equality — yet nothing in my world seemed to be changing. The walls of prejudice and separation were firmly in place in these small Oklahoma towns. Could it ever change?

Once I was discussing this unchanging wall of prejudice with my mother. I told her, "I'm going to quit making these speeches, Mama. We talk and talk but don't seem to get anything done."

Whenever I received an invitation Mama always encouraged me to go. She told me, "What rich opportunities you have, Phillip. I didn't have these opportunities, and your daddy didn't have these invitations. Many other black people haven't been invited, but you have been selected. You need to go and take advantage of it and do all of the speaking that you can." My mother encouraged me to have a vision for breaking down the walls in our relationships. This vision for reaching across the walls has carried me for many years.

FORGIVENESS DESPITE THE PAIN

As a teenager of about fifteen I went with my dad into an IGA Grocery store located some distance from the Negro district. My dad bent down to select an item from a bottom shelf when a white man came up behind him and kicked him — a solid boot in the backside! My dad was a good-sized man at around 250 pounds.

When Dad was kicked I was shocked but waited to see what he would do about it. He straightened up slowly and deliberately, then turned toward the assailant. The man blurted out that he had wanted to "kick his butt" for a long time. I could sense the feelings of anger starting to swell in my chest. In my mind I was ready to square off with the guy. With both my dad and me there, we could put a hurt on this guy. I said, "Daddy, aren't you going to do something?"

But my dad looked the guy straight on with strength and poise then said, "As long as you're a white guy and I'm a black man, don't you ever raise your foot and kick me again."

Then my dad turned to me and said, "Come on, son. We're getting out of here." I was pained because I wanted to wear that guy out on the floor. But my dad and I walked out to the car. As we rode down the street I asked, "Dad, why? He had no right to treat you like that!"

"I know he had no right, son," Dad said. He explained to me that guys like that man didn't see us as people. They were ignorant and afraid. These types of experiences gave us a clear-cut choice for action. We could be angry and bitter, or we could forgive them because they didn't know what they were doing. We could leave that hurt with God. The Maker of the universe would carry the offense for us and leave us free in our spirits. Through that experience Dad taught me the value of forgiveness in the midst of our pain.

We have a biblical example of this type of action from the Lord Jesus. Jesus was subjected to one of the most painful deaths possible. The soldiers pounded spikes into both of Jesus' hands then into His feet. After the nails were in place, the soldiers lifted the cross into an upright position and dropped it into a hole. The jarring drop shook every bone in His body. The Gospel of Luke makes this observation:

> There were also two others, criminals, led with Him to be put to death. And when they had come to the place called Calvary, there they crucified Him, and the criminals, one on the right hand and the other on the left. Then Jesus said, "Father, forgive them, for they do not know what they do." And they divided His garments and cast lots (23:32-34).

In His pain on the cross Jesus watched the soldiers

gamble for His clothing. While the blood dripped from His hands, feet and back, He had the strength of character to pray for His persecutors and ask His heavenly Father to forgive them.

As we work on this issue of prejudice and reconciliation in our lives, people will often revile us and give us additional pain. Like my dad we will unexpectedly get our "butts kicked." The natural response is to double our fists and look for a means of revenge. As believers in Christ and people who have God's Spirit inside us we are instead to turn and offer forgiveness. Then the bitterness won't grow inside, and we can be free in God's Spirit to receive His creative ideas for corrective action.

THE VALUE OF PAIN IN A RELATIONSHIP

No one wants pain — physical or emotional. Yet if we commit to breaking down the walls between us, we will experience pain. Several years ago, I experienced unexpected pain from a couple of my white friends in Denver.

Through my radio program, *It's Prayer Time*, aired, I met Pastor Francine.* She is white, and I'm black. We both had hearts for the work of the Lord. We decided to meet together and have remained close friends.

About the same time Francine met Paul,* a professional man. Before long they were married, and I was in their wedding party.

As a man of means Paul could support Francine's ministry. From the first day that Francine introduced

*Names have been changed for the privacy of those involved.

me to Paul I could sense a little reservation in him, but I wasn't sure if there was any meaning behind it.

Over the years Francine and I preached in the same services. We traveled together and followed each other on the radio. Our families built a close relationship. Francine's daughters called me uncle and I called them my nieces.

A couple of years ago Paul got very sick and was hospitalized, and I went to see him. He wasn't quite himself because of the illness. I walked into the hospital room and said, "Hey, brother. How are you doing?"

Paul looked up at me and said, "Oh, you little black nigger. You've been hanging around our family for a long time. I want to tell you, little nigger, that you don't belong to us." His words stung me. Immediately I knew that this attitude had been the cause of Paul's reservation around me over the years. These words came from his sick subconsciousness, but they were as strong as a lashing from a whip.

Because of my long-term relationship with the family, I was able to move past those words, and today, continue my relationship with them. But I walked out of the hospital room feeling dumb-founded, angry and broken. At first I planned to tell Francine about the incident. Then I considered it again and decided she didn't need that.

As a woman pastor Francine faced her share of difficulties from other pastors. In some ways I've been slow about receiving women pastors as well, but not Francine. I always maintained my relationship with her. Francine loves God and God's people. As I bore the brunt of Paul's resentment I had to work through a lot of pain.

When we experience pain from a situation like this we have a choice. Do we confront the person who inflicted the pain? In some cases the answer is yes. In those cases we return to that person and go over why the relationship was broken. Before we go back to the person we need to seek God's wisdom for our words and not enter into the conversation with hot anger or a temper. If we have strong emotion behind our words then the confrontation will not be productive and will probably evolve into further pain for the relationship. We need to move with caution and carefully consider the ramifications when we decide to confront such pain in a relationship.

Yet at other times, such as this situation with Francine and Paul, the response of wisdom is not to confront the person. Instead I took my pain to the throne of God.

If pain has entered your life from a broken relationship then maybe you need to turn to God. Ask God to touch your heart for this person in a fresh way and heal the brokenness. I believe God will construct both time and place to deal properly with these unhealthy aspects of a relationship.

Sometimes you can't return to the person who has inflicted the pain. At other times it's not wise to return to the person. As believers in Jesus Christ we have a great resource in the power and strength of the Holy Spirit. God's Spirit can touch our hearts and restore us.

MY WAKE-UP CALL FOR RECONCILIATION

Reconciliation will not be a simple process; it will

be costly. For each person the cost will be different. For some it will be financial. For others it will be emotional.

In 1973 I made a decision that cost in terms of finances for my family. I chose to resign from my part-time jobs and go into full-time ministry. God began to add men to my church, and consequently we increased the number of families in attendance.

Reportedly when the woman in a family becomes a Christian, then about 35 to 40 percent of the family will also become Christians. When the man trusts Christ and becomes a Christian then the percentage of the family to become Christians increases to about 65 or 70 percent. But when both the woman and the man make a personal commitment to Christ, then the percentage increases to 95 to 98 percent.

With our renewed commitment to families our congregation grew. We outgrew the building purchased in 1969 that seated only about 150 people. We managed to purchase a large building with a seven-hundred-seat auditorium. We had a lot of pride in the location of our building at the corner of Kalamath and Tenth.

Because this was a main thoroughfare of the city, hundreds of thousands of cars drove past that corner every week and saw our large marquee. I was changing that sign every day. I worked hard to make sure that sign sounded good and that my name was underneath it, "Dr. Phillip H. Porter, Jr." (I received an honorary doctorate degree from Trinity Hall College and Seminary in 1971.) I wanted every-one to know that we had arrived!

In our journeys of reconciliation, God wants us to

keep focused on Him — no matter what comes into our lives. Detractors and interruptions will try to steer us away from God and toward ourselves, our accomplishments, self-worth and values. Unfortunately I had taken my eyes off Christ. Instead I was promoting myself.

I lost my focus of reaching all denominations and was gearing up to return to a more denominational or parochial perspective on my ministry. I named our church All Nations for a purpose, but I temporarily ignored that purpose. My focus was on becoming the bishop for Colorado within my denomination, the Church of God in Christ.

That year at the denomination's annual convocation in Memphis I went seeking the position of bishop for Colorado, and I lost the election. As the votes were counted I prayed, "Dear Lord, if I don't get to be appointed bishop of the state, please give me the city of Denver. I will be satisfied." But I was not chosen.

Feeling forlorn and discouraged, I prepared to return to Denver. The night before the meetings concluded I fell into a dream that puzzled me, and I woke up wondering what it meant. I could see my church building, and it was on fire. An Egyptian sphinx rose out of the ashes of my church. The sphinx stood firm like a monument of the burnt rubbish of my church.

Suddenly I woke up from the dream. I picked up my Bible and began to search through Scripture. Throughout most of the night, I prayed and reflected on the significance of it. From my research emerged a sermon titled: "Up Out of the Ashes." When I returned to my church the following Sunday, I preached that message. I thought the vision was a message about losing the position of bishop for Colorado. My interpretation was that God would raise me up from my loss and give me a strong ministry. So I preached this sermon to my congregation.

Two days after I preached I learned the real significance of my dream. During the night our church caught on fire. An old coal-burning furnace which had been converted into natural gas had given us trouble with the pilot light even though the repairs had been done. That night the burner got stuck on high and never shut off. It overheated the area and caught on fire.

We lost everything in a five-alarm fire in which three firemen were injured.

Help Across Racial Lines

As we dug through the ashes of our church, the congregation came together in a fresh and wonderful way. In order to rebuild we needed each other. From December to April we raised fifty thousand dollars for a new building through community projects and personal commitments. As we searched for a new building, we wanted a larger one for our growing congregation.

Before the fire God allowed our congregation a great opportunity to begin a wonderful relationship with the pastor and members of a Southern Baptist church located only one block from our now burnt-out church home. This congregation joyfully opened their doors to us and shared their facilities while we searched for a new building. What a tremendous four months we enjoyed, staggering our services to accommodate each other. I had never imagined a Southern Baptist church of predominately Hispanic makeup would allow a predominately black Holiness congregation to share their facilities. We learned to receive from others. This period also stretched our capacity for serving their needs.

While we were sharing the facilities at the Southern Baptist church, the chairman of our building committee located an available site in Denver owned by Faith Bible Chapel. It was located at Ninth and Acoma in the downtown area.

This old church building had been vacant for about a year. Initially Faith Bible Chapel had a contract on the building for it to be turned into office space. But their desire was for the building to remain a church. In March 1980 I walked into the building and saw the beauty of the sanctuary. The late Kathryn Kuhlman had remodeled this old livery stable into a church for her ministry during the 1930s, and it contained a fifteen-hundred-seat auditorium. My heart melted before the Lord, and I prayed, "Oh, God, if we could purchase this building then I would be so grateful."

The committee chairman and I fell at the altar, and I prayed, "God, is it possible? I don't know how it will be possible. We don't have $358,000." That was the asking price.

In prayer the Lord showed me a price to offer, the monthly payment and the length of the contract. When I got up off my knees I turned to our building chairman and said, "I'm going to offer them $250,000 for the church."

His mouth dropped open, and he stared at me in disbelief. "Pastor Porter, I told you that they have a contract on this building for $358,000. You don't want to buy a building. You've just got us out here wasting our time!"

"Then I'm going to offer them $275,000," I said.

"I'm going home," he retorted. "I'm not going to fool with you."

We left the building, but later I called the leaders at Faith Bible Chapel, introduced myself and told them about my interest in their building. We met at a local restaurant. I told them about how the Lord had spoken to me.

They listened to the offer, then went to their church. About an hour later they called me and said, "We'll accept your offer of $275,000 with one condition. You need to allow us to give you five thousand dollars back to help repair the leak in the roof." We concluded the contract for the church. This was such a great beginning to what has become a longstanding, intercultural, interracial and interdenominational relationship.

Faith Bible Chapel has helped our congregation in many ways. They saw our offer as a tremendous opportunity to build a bridge to brethren within the African American community and help us acquire a significant piece of property. Since that time we have maintained a tremendous relationship. Whenever I see George Morrison, the pastor, we have a great kinship — like brothers. Pastor Morrison also serves on the board of directors for

Promise Keepers. Because of our relationship I can talk with this brother in Christ about anything.

Recently they invited us over to their church for another one of our many exchanges and gave us a significant seed offering for our ministry. Our drama team presented a sterling performance of *Sermons in the Negro Dialect* for them.

Faith Bible Chapel has a tremendous impact on the Denver community. In some ways our church is an additional arm of their ministry. One day I turned to George and said, "Brother George, we should just merge our congregations together."

He looked at me thoughtfully and then smiled, "Maybe it would work." A predominately white congregation reached out to our church and helped us rise from the ashes to reach all nations. We haven't merged our congregations, but Faith Bible Chapel has been an important partner in our ministry of reconciliation.

Seven years earlier when I struggled with whether or not to go into full-time ministry, the Lord said, "Trust Me, and I will increase your ministry tenfold." I stepped out in faith, and the Lord fulfilled His promise — in only seven years. Even the increase in the number of seats, from 150 to 1,500, was an indicator of how God restored our vision and property tenfold. At our auditorium people from all races came to worship and left to serve.

THE WALL OF DENOMINATIONS

"Where do you go to church?" Sometimes people will ask me that question. I'm sure they expect that

I will reply with a denomination label. If you ask this question and expect a denominational answer maybe you are building a denominational wall in your life.

Consider your relationships with friends, acquaintances, neighbors and coworkers. Do you relate well only to those who attend your church? It's fairly easy to hide behind the label of "charismatic" or "Baptist" or "Catholic" or "Episcopal."

As the Lord enlarged my vision to include people from various denominations, it broke down an important wall. For years my focus was on my denominational affiliation to the exclusion of the rest of the body of Christ. I put up a wall in my own life instead of moving to break it down.

A denomination in and of itself isn't bad. But we cannot allow the denomination to cause us to exclude parts of the body of Christ. I let my denominational affiliation perpetrate racism in my actions.

From an early age within the Church of God in Christ I had been taught an exclusive-type attitude. Our thoughts ran something like this: "As a black person I may be struggling now, but my eyes are focused on heaven. I'm going to spend eternity with the Lord Jesus. And those white devils who mistreat us in the name of Jesus as well as those sectarian folks — they are going to face an eternity in hell." During the 1930s and 1940s this sort of segregated attitude allowed us to hang on and get through those difficult days and nights.

In those days every place had signs that said "white only" or "no coloreds allowed." We sat in the back of buses and had access only through the rear doors of restaurants. At the movie houses we sat in "our place" — the balcony. We figured that white people were going to hell. Where else would they spend eternity when they treated us in this manner? We knew they were hell-bound.

We couldn't fight back and win, so we simply didn't fight back. In the small towns of Oklahoma during the 1930s and 1940s black men were incarcerated and lynched without ever being given a trial. What's more disturbing is that even since I left Oklahoma in the late 1950s there have been mysterious deaths of young black males in that state.

The same attitudes white men held in the past toward black men have carried over to today's society. Although it was a fair trial, the recent not-guilty verdict from the O. J. Simpson case left many white people dissatisfied. This reaction was nothing new to the African American community. Since we didn't even receive trials in the past — much less fair ones — we figure what's the point in expecting white people to understand and be satisfied with the verdict from this trial?

Because of my personal relationship with Christ I pressed beyond the persecution and prejudice of my past. Through my life I have met and become friends with many wonderful white people with great hearts.

Let's go back to the question, "Where do you go to church?" My first answer is, "I'm a Christian, and I love the Lord Jesus." When I present this relationship in a foundational way, it doesn't throw up any denominational walls. Instead I can and do fellowship across denominational lines. I maintain strong relationships within my denomination of the Church of God in Christ but relate to brothers and sisters in Christ from a variety of churches. Our bond is in Christ, and we need continually to lower the walls of denominationalism.

"LORD, NOT IN A BAPTIST CHURCH"

I grew up as a third generation Church of God in Christ youngster. Early in my life I was exposed to many religious persuasions. I spoke in a variety of churches and community meetings. At age nineteen I answered a call to the gospel ministry in the summer of 1956.

That summer I went to my uncle's farm in northeastern Oklahoma to work. When I arrived I told my uncle about my decision to preach. My uncle worked as a lay youth minister on the staff of First Baptist Church of Nowata, Oklahoma. He said to me, "Great, I'm glad the Lord gave you a call to the gospel ministry, Phil. I want you to bring the message to our youth meeting this summer."

In my very parochial way I protested saying, "I can't do that." In my mind I was firmly entrenched in the Church of God in Christ. I couldn't preach my first sermon in a Baptist church. My reputation would be tarnished forever!

My uncle insisted on scheduling the event; it was about a month away. I agonized over the meeting, and I studied and prayed. During this month my uncle asked me, "How are you coming, Phil, on preparing your message?"

Every time I told him, "I can't do it, Uncle."

He brought a halt to my protest saying, "Oh,

yeah? Well, you've got to do it." Out of respect for my uncle I worked on my sermon. The day before I was scheduled to speak I rode in from the fields on my uncle's tractor. He said, "Well, son, how are you doing? You know tomorrow is your big day."

I said, "I told you I cannot do that."

He said, "Oh, yeah, you've got to speak. We've got the word out, and everybody is expecting you to preach. As a matter of fact, take the rest of the day off, go up to your room and get yourself together. I've got some books in there that will help you."

Inside I was distraught and emotionally torn about preaching a sermon in the Baptist church. I went to my room in the attic of the house. I took a couple of my uncle's books and sat there. I still couldn't get anything to say at the service.

While reading and praying I turned to the Lord and said, "Dear God, maybe I missed You. Maybe You didn't call me to the ministry after all. Lord it seems so odd and strange and off base for me, a Holiness boy, to be preaching to a Baptist congregation for my first official message. Something is wrong with that, Lord!" I was trying to convince the Lord about the wrongness of this scheduled meeting, not fully understanding that God works in mysterious ways.

Finally I created a solution to my problem. I told the Lord, "God, I'll even get up there tomorrow morning and tell them that I made a mistake. I wasn't called to preach there. God, please don't let me preach that sermon."

While I was praying I had a strong image come to my mind. I saw myself climbing a long set of stairs like those outside a state capital building. I climbed a step then did a task that was required. After I finished my task on a step there would be a great applause.

Then I climbed another step and went in front of another audience. When I finished speaking the crowd gave me another round of applause. As I continued to think about this image, it was almost as if I were viewing stages of my life. Each step of my life I did something in front of other people. I continued climbing until I reached the very top.

This lofty point was the highest I could go. As with the other steps I did what the Lord required of me. My performance was impeccable, and I knew it was. I finished, and strangely, the crowd was silent. There was no applause. No one had applauded throughout this great performance.

Finally I took a bow. The curtain closed while I was bowing. I remained bowed for a while — waiting for some applause. I couldn't understand why no one applauded.

With tears in my eyes and heart, I was stunned. I knew I had given my best performance, but no one applauded. I stood there for what seemed like an eternity, but it was only five minutes or so. I started to raise myself from the bowed position. Just as I raised up, from behind the curtain a great applause broke through. People clapped, whistled and yelled, "Come back. Encore. Return."

It felt so marvelous to hear such applause. With great excitement I tried to find the opening in the curtain to get back to the crowd for an encore performance. But I could not find any way to get through. My performance was finished. There would be no encore.

As I thought about it I felt the Lord was saying to me, "Your life will be one where you are called to do what is required, and serve people — at any level — until you reach the top. The real applause and importance of your life won't come until the end."

This perspective was comforting to me because I knew I was in the hands of the Lord. I also felt that my job was to go ahead and preach the sermon in the Baptist church. So this Pentecostal boy preached his first message in a Baptist church.

That sermon set a course for me across denominational lines, and I've never looked back. My first real summer job came the next summer. I was a camp counselor for the Disciples of Christ. Such a step was only the beginning.

When I finally came to Denver in 1963 for my ordination, it was held in a Christian Methodist Episcopal church. Our state meeting was using those facilities at the time.

So at an early age I was asked to preach my first official message at a Baptist church, served in a Disciples of Christ summer camp and had my ordination services at a CME church. My life is a wonderful saga that God ordained so that I would be ready to be used as chairman of the board of directors of Promise Keepers. He began preparing me to break down the denominational walls through these early steps in my life, teaching me what reconciliation was all about.

POINTS TO PONDER

1. Revisit my story in the opening pages of this chapter. Imagine yourself in my shoes as a young teenager preaching in an all-white church.

   ✓ Would you have the necessary courage to take such an action?

   It will take conscious acts of courage and risk for the walls to fall down. It will not always be popular or easy. Talk with a friend about your own willingness to take such steps.

2. Now put yourself in the place of the two women from the WCTU. They felt ashamed of their own race and the actions against me, an African American. Yet these women exhibited courage and willingness to go against the majority. Sometimes we will have to go against the majority in order for reconciliation to become a reality.

   ✓ Pray and ask God to give you the necessary boldness and wisdom to tear down the walls around you. Then listen as the Lord guides and speaks to your heart, and take the directed actions.

3. My childhood experience of worship with different races gives me hope for a

future of reconciliation. Think about the experiences you have had with people from different backgrounds or races, maybe at a Promise Keepers conference or another meeting.

✓ How do these experiences give you hope for changing the world around you?

4. My dad taught me an unforgettable lesson about forgiveness when he was kicked in a grocery store. In our journey to reconciliation sometimes we will be misunderstood and even experience pain from others (whether emotional or physical).

✓ If you've had these types of painful experiences, how did you handle them?

✓ Did you learn to forgive or did you allow the seeds of bitterness to be planted in your heart?

✓ How can you uproot of the seeds of bitterness?

If you've not had painful experiences in the journey of reconciliation, get ready. The apostle Paul wrote Timothy some sobering words in 2 Timothy 3:12-13, "Yes, and all who desire to live godly in Christ Jesus will suffer persecution. But evil men and impostors will grow worse and worse, deceiving and being deceived."

✓ When you do endure painful experiences, are you prepared to forgive your persecutor?

✓ Plan how you will act now before the situation occurs.

Sometimes painful experiences come from unexpected sources. For example, I thought I had a good relationship with Pastor Francine's husband, Paul. Only when Paul was ill did I discover his true feelings, and it was painful. I took my pain to God's throne and asked for His healing in my life.

✓ If you've been through such pain, ask for God's restoration in your life and heart.

5. How do you hear a wake-up call for reconciliation? For me, it took a burning church. Your wake-up call could come from reading about and learning from the experiences of others.

✓ What sort of wake-up call have you had in your own life?

✓ Evaluate the personal cost in your journey of reconciliation.

6. I struggled with crossing a denominational barrier when I prepared to preach my first sermon. The Lord showed me we are all the same in the body of Christ.

✓ Do you have walls of denomination-alism in your life?

✓ Have you been taught that your denomination is the best (as I was taught) and everyone else is bound for hell?

✓ What steps can you take to break down this wall in your life?

✓ When you talk with a friend or neighbor about Christ do you empha-size your church or your personal relationship with Jesus?

Your response to this last question may reveal your tendency toward building the wall of denominationalism.

CHAPTER 4

FEELING THE PAIN

There are no simple answers when it comes to understanding each other. It takes time and energy. Before you begin a journey of reconciliation you need to ask yourself, "Am I willing to share the pain and past hurts of the other person?"

Pain? Don't quit reading right now! No one wants to experience pain. Yet reconciliation means accepting and submitting to another's pain.

Suppose I say something sharp to a member of my congregation. (We'll call him John.) I don't realize my words came across as sharp, but they truly hurt John. During the next few days John takes time to think about what I said. Taking a deep breath John asks for an appointment to meet with me but gives me no clue about the subject for this meeting.

When he walks into the room, I can tell John has a weighty matter to discuss. Is it his family? Or his work? No.

To my surprise it is me. John says, "Pastor, the other day your words came across to me as sharp and stinging. It hurt me when you said _____."

I listen to John and say, "Well, I had no idea that my words would affect you like that. In fact, I haven't thought about that incident at all." I don't immediately ask for his forgiveness, but as I think about what John has expressed, I discover that I too carry resentment about this incident. Instead of resolving it I became busy with a different activity in order to repress my feelings. Now with this confrontation from John my pain resurfaces again.

John watches impatiently as I process his words, then he says with disgust, "Well, just forget it. I sense no forgiveness from you. We can't be reconciled." With a look of bewilderment I watch as John stomps out of the room.

What was that all about? Did John want to be reconciled to me? He acted like it, but when it came right down to it, no, John didn't want to go through any process of reconciliation.

From John's perspective he attempted reconciliation. But in reality he took the initial step then quit because he wasn't willing to accept that I also was hurt as a result of this incident. Real reconciliation takes time, energy and effort to understand the sources of pain and the willingness to share it.

Often our world tries to put Band-Aids on racial prejudice instead of honestly facing our past. Are we willing to look beyond our surface differences and understand each other? It costs.

Some people may ask, "Why do we have to face the pain of our past? Can't we deal with the here and now without facing the past?" The answer is no. Each of us is a product of our past. The opportunities or lack of opportunities we have comes from our background.

Consider Others' Pain

Let's consider the case of slavery and its various nuances. Present-day white Americans must realize the repercussions of past actions. Because of the privileges afforded their race, white Americans have become the leaders of the world; they are the most educated and have the most power in our society. How did this happen and at what price?

Our country was built on hard work, commitment and accomplishment. When the English settlers arrived in the country they met the Native Americans. These Native Americans were willing to share their secrets for living in this country and for raising crops. If some of these Native Americans were unwilling to help, then their lives were forfeited. Essentially the Native American was a stepping stone for the white American. They moved ahead and conquered the country at the expense of Native Americans.

Into the foundation stone of the white American

was etched a commitment to put God first in their lives and to seek a place of worship. Their message to the Native American was: cooperate, give up your land or get killed. America's forefathers decided to work the land, but they needed indentured servants from overseas. They went abroad to Africa and brought slaves to this country.

A significant part of becoming a slave meant the African had to give up his identity, his name, his culture and his self-worth. Each virtue that he gave up in his slavery amounted to a part of his dehumanization. These Africans were self-willed and strong people. For them to give up their humanity wasn't a simple process.

The African male was a designated storyteller. The pride of his life was to tell stories and pass along history to younger generations. But as a slave he lost this storytelling ability and forfeited his music, culture and creativity. His family was torn apart, separated and sold. In the new world of the United States, this grown man became a laborer or "boy" who could never become a man. The dehumanization process took years and many steps to bring down the African American man to such a low level.

The understanding of this dehumanization process helps us identify the pain associated with reconciliation. We must put forth the effort to understand the journey of other people and their ancestors in order to be reconciled to each other as brothers and sisters in Christ.

The African American, the Hispanic and the Native American were treated as less than human beings during the early years of America. Each of these groups was inferior to the whites in the areas of opportunity to worship, housing, living conditions, education and even nutrition. They were not properly compensated for their work.

As you have this background and history of the races in mind, you can begin to glimpse the difficulty of racial reconciliation. A white person comes to me and wants to be reconciled. He tells me, "I've worked through the past and pain. Jesus Christ is in my life, and let's be brothers."

I ask the person, "Can you feel the pain of my past? Do you understand how we are different?" Until this person comes face-to-face with the reality of my past, it's difficult for him to be reconciled. We can learn about the reconciliation process from the life of Zacchaeus in the New Testament.

THE ZACCHEAN PRINCIPLE

I've drawn a lot of strength through the years from what I call the Zacchean Principle. Even small children know and love the story of Zacchaeus.

In Luke 19 we learn Zacchaeus was a man with a sharp dichotomy in his life. While he was small in stature, Zacchaeus was the chief among tax collectors. With solid infighting techniques the small man had gnawed and clawed his way to the top of the social ladder. One rung at a time he had climbed to the top of his tax collector profession. Even though Zacchaeus was at the top of his game, he wasn't happy. The Bible says that he was "disturbed."

News traveled fast throughout the region of Jericho. Jesus was coming to town!

Jesus is a lowly Nazarene. He doesn't have any social standing, Zacchaeus thought. *Yet He commands the attention of people from all walks of life. Even the children follow Jesus. Why?*

Zacchaeus heard that Jesus would be coming by. He had to see this man named Jesus. *What does Jesus have that I don't have?* he wondered. Despite his riches, Zacchaeus knew that he didn't have a large following like Jesus.

To get a bird's-eye look at the Nazarene, Zacchaeus climbed up into a sycamore tree. He thought that he was the only one who was looking for Jesus Christ. When Jesus walked near the tree where Zacchaeus was perched, He looked up. Jesus said, "Zacchaeus, make haste and come down, for today I must stay at your house" (Luke 19:5).

Jesus' decision to go to the house of the chief tax collector wasn't popular. Immediately the people muttered against Jesus saying, "He's gone to be a guest with a man who is a sinner" (v. 7).

But because of the presence of Jesus in his home and now in his life, Zacchaeus changed his life direction. It didn't take preaching or a special miracle; instead Zacchaeus was overwhelmed with the magnitude and power of Jesus Christ. He climbed out of the tree and gladly welcomed Jesus.

Zacchaeus was immediately transformed! He told Jesus in Luke 19:8:

> Look, Lord, I give half of my goods to the poor; and if I have taken anything from any-

one by false accusation, I restore fourfold.

The Lord Jesus recognized that Zacchaeus was a changed man. Jesus said:

> Today salvation has come to this house, because he also is a son of Abraham; for the Son of Man has come to seek and to save that which was lost (vv. 9-10).

When the presence of Jesus is in our lives, then we change. In the area of reconciliation Jesus must be in our lives. When He is in the house (our physical bodies and our inner souls), then He gives us the means for total change. He gives us a compassion for the poor and turns our greed into giving. That is why I call this the Zacchean Principle or the changing power of Jesus Christ. Our changing is based on the fact that we have a personal relationship with the Savior.

As we are willing to come into a personal relationship with people who are different from us, we put ourselves in the path of reconciliation.

MINISTER TO THE WHOLE MAN

In the presence of Jesus Zacchaeus recognized that he had become rich by cheating people when he collected taxes. With this new insight Zacchaeus restored money to those he cheated.

As we understand the wrongs of the past in race relations, we will take steps to share our resources across racial lines. We will take steps to help our brothers with economic and social matters.

Our natural inclination is to rebel against these ideas. We can't do it — unless we are empowered by love from Jesus Christ. When we operate with this spiritual power, we can give up *our* plans and *our* desires and lay them at the feet of Jesus.

Racial reconciliation can't be done in partiality but must be a treatment of the whole man. Such steps will not be easily accomplished in one day or one meeting. It takes a lifelong commitment to the process of reconciliation. We need to come alongside people from other races so we can share our resources, talents and abilities.

The Frog in the Kettle

The changes from reconciliation in our culture will in most cases occur gradually. If you place a frog in cold water, you can slowly raise the temperature until the kettle boils. The frog won't jump out or even notice that the temperature is rising. But if the frog is thrown into a kettle of boiling water, it will try to escape. The frog has found the temperature change too sudden.

When it comes to racial reconciliation, changes in our world will occur in the same way. We need to show our brothers and sisters how to blend in the world. Then all of us can share the abundant life that Christ promised in John 10:10.

> The thief does not come except to steal, and to kill, and to destroy. I have come that they may have life, and that they may have it more abundantly.

One of my closest white friends is Gordon England. In 1992 I met this former Evangelical Free Church pastor, missionary and seminary professor as a part of the board of directors for Promise Keepers. When we talked together, Gordon shifted the conversation from friendly and casual chit-chat to more serious topics. He asked me, "Have you had any pain with integration?"

When I thought about it for a few minutes, some new emotions swelled to the surface. For the first time in thirty years I remembered the rejection of my social work application in Walsenburg, Colorado. I had buried my feelings about that particular portion of my life, but Gordon's question returned them to the surface. I began to choke back my tears.

Gordon drew close to me and put his arm around my shoulder. "Bishop, that rejection really hurt you."

"Yes," I said. Then Gordon encouraged my tears and asked me to share about that time in my life. The experience drew us closer as brothers in Christ, but gradually I began to pull back. I thought, *I don't want to be this vulnerable. I've got to pull myself together.* I took my pain and shoved it back into a drawer in my heart. Maybe I wouldn't have to look at it again for another thirty years.

But Gordon sensed the need to share my experience, and he wouldn't let go. As he continued to pursue a relationship with me, I grew more and more comfortable with our friendship. I allowed myself to be more open and transparent with him. The experience has fostered a good relationship.

Gordon is one of the few white friends who knows he can drop by my house whenever he feels like it. In fact, he recently arrived at my house near midnight.

When Gordon learned that my youngest daughter, Phyllis, had been in a car accident he was concerned about her neck and back pain. The next day Gordon gave Phyllis a call. "I know what you must be going through, Phyllis," Gordon said. "Several years ago I had whiplash from an accident, and my hot tub was exactly what I needed. Why don't you come over and use our tub?"

Phyllis listened politely but didn't accept the invitation. While I lead a relatively large congregation in Denver, our family tends to be private about our personal lives. "That white man wants me to come and use his hot tub," Phyllis told me.

Gordon didn't make the offer once and forget it. Instead he has called three or four times and encouraged Phyllis to get the help from the warm water. Before too long I suspect Phyllis will take advantage of this gracious offer from Gordon.

Racial reconciliation doesn't come with one or two attempts. Gordon has set his sights on the long-term goal. He has said to himself, "I'm committed to the Porter family and the process of helping them. I'm going to get it done."

Another part of the attitude for reconciliation is that you can't turn back. Jeremiah 30:24 says:

> The fierce anger of the Lord will not turn back until he fully accomplishes the purposes of his heart. In days to come you will understand this (NIV).

While this passage is in the context of God's anger toward the sins of Israel, it points out a characteristic of God — He doesn't turn back. The heart of God constantly reaches out to man.

We imitate this characteristic of God in the process of reconciliation. Our plans and goals remain constantly in our hearts, and we have the dedication of a call from God. We say to God, "I can do nothing greater, so here I am, Lord."

A Personal Hero

One of my personal heroes in the movement of reconciliation is Coach Bill McCartney. As Coach says, "Racial reconciliation is a war. There are no wars without casualties." Leaving a lucrative job as the head coach for the University of Colorado football team, Bill took severe financial cuts to devote his time to Promise Keepers. When he heard the call of God in his life he obeyed, even in the area of racial reconciliation.

During the last several months Coach and his wife, Lyndi, have been living out this call with different leaders in the African American community. For several days the McCartneys have lived with leaders like Dr. and Mrs. E. V. Hill, Tony and Lois Evans, and John and Vera Mae Perkins.

From the first time Coach Mac came to my church, he was a man who was strong in a cause and a purpose yet was weak when faced with his own failures and lack of insight. Coach was willing to humble himself with other men. Yet he is never so vulnerable as on his knees with his hands outstretched to God and tears streaming down his face. For us to be racially reconciled, it will take a transparency and ability to be weak with our brothers in Christ.

Repeatedly Bill McCartney is sounding the call to men, "We've got to feel the pain of other men — the black, the Native American and the Hispanic — before we can minister to them." He tells the people in the inner cities, "I want to feel your pain and minister to your pain, but you too must come along and take responsibility." The black and other racial communities must raise up leaders and support them in this process of bearing responsibility.

Several years ago Coach Mac attended the funeral of a former University of Colorado football player. This African American player had graduated from CU and had become a lawyer. At the service Coach Mac heard crying, singing and the message of the minister. He felt the deep sorrow of the people. This was an unusual experience for him. The sorrow was not just for their lost friend but for the lost potential. Here was a young man who was gifted, yet because of death he would never come to know his full potential.

Coach Mac spoke at the funeral and expressed how he identified with the pain. "I've felt pain and separation as well because of the long hours that I put in my career instead of my family. Now as I think about that separation, it brings me great sorrow," he said.

A few years later, Coach was speaking in another city and again expressed the pain he felt caused by his choices in life. Afterward an elderly African American man walked up to Coach Mac and waved a bony finger in his face then pointed it at his chest and screamed, "You don't know pain. You think you have pain. You ought to know my pain. My grandparents were slaves and were beaten. I've run my finger over the scars on their whipped backs. We were called names like Jim Crow and the N-word. We had to use segregated restrooms, drinking fountains and restaurants. We were spit on and pushed aside. You don't know anything about pain, Coach."

Coach Mac listened patiently to the elderly man, then said, "You're right. I don't know anything about that pain which you know. But now I have been made more aware of it because you shared those stories with me."

We must share the hard experiences of the past if we are to move ahead and make progress in racial reconciliation. The historical reality is present, and we must recognize it as the first step toward healing.

Solomon prayed on behalf of Israel in 2 Chronicles 6. The king pleaded for forgiveness for the sins of the people which was necessary if God were to indeed bless Israel. Solomon became a bridge between the sins of the people and a holy God.

This same type of bridge building has to occur in racial reconciliation. Only then can we become a bridge between what has been and what will be in the future. We need to understand where each race has come from historically. That takes sharing the mistakes of the past. Then we can love each other only after we've gone through that purification process.

We think about purification in terms of gold. In

order to purify gold the dross is burned off the precious metal. This imagery is used in 1 Peter 1:22.

> Since you have purified your souls in obeying the truth through the Spirit in sincere love of the brethren, love one another fervently with a pure heart.

As Coach obeys the truth, his love for others increases. Coach Mac has purpose and calling yet realizes that he needs to be transparent and vulnerable with brothers.

PART OF WHY COACH MAC "FEELS THE PAIN"

Coach Mac has done more than simply meet with people, listen and then speak to gatherings of men, large and small. Coach has walked a journey of pain. His passion for reconciliation springs from some deep personal experiences.

In the fall of 1988 Kristy, the McCartneys' only daughter, fell in love with Sal Aunese, a Hawaiian quarterback on the CU team. In the spring Kristy gave birth to Sal's son out of wedlock. Five months after the birth, Sal died of cancer. Coach didn't speak publicly of the grandson until the memorial service. There Coach Mac praised his daughter for not having an abortion, and he continued to be supportive of her.

In the spring of 1992 Kristy again dated a CU football player, an African American defensive tackle from New Orleans named Shannon Clavelle. She gave birth to a second son out of wedlock.

In the face of media coverage of their daughter Coach Mac and his wife remained supportive of Kristy.

The pain from these two relationships with people from other races sent Coach on a soul search and into a deep experience with God. It has melted his heart so that he reaches out and touches people from all walks of life.

Instead of hiding the experience Coach has taken this personal difficulty and used it for God's glory. It has pushed Coach into the forefront of the movement of breaking down the walls for reconciliation.

ONLY THROUGH GOD

It may look simply impossible to share another person's pain. It is only through the power of Jesus Christ that we can share with another person their experience. God showed us the way for this experience through His Son Jesus Christ.

When Jesus took off His robes of heaven's glory, He came to earth as a baby in Bethlehem. Born of human flesh from a woman He took this drastic action to give mankind a means to reach God.

Through His horrible death on the cross Jesus, although without sin, took on the sin and therefore the pain of the world. It was God in Christ who reconciled the world to Himself. In the same way, when God lives in us through the Holy Spirit, we can be reconciled to each other (2 Cor. 5:18-20). Without the power of the Holy Spirit in our lives and without a connection to the heavenly Father, we can't own each other's pain.

NOT JUST ONE DIRECTION

Owning one another's pain isn't done in just one direction. It's not just the whites who need to own the pain of the African American community. The African Americans also need to own the pain of the whites.

African Americans have to reach out to the whites who live in this "now" generation, people who have no awareness of the bitterness of the history of African Americans. They can't identify with the depth of the hurt of the past. Our white brothers and sisters want to have African American friends. They want to have relationships that reach across the races.

African Americans are reluctant to reach out to their white brothers. It's because they haven't sat down with a white person and heard him say, "But I'm different. I wouldn't have had slaves or treated you differently. You don't know me. Don't feel that way toward me. Why hate me? Why don't you like me?" Can you sense the pain in these questions from the white community?

As African Americans consider it, we now understand and say, "Wow, I'm still holding something against these people today. Why don't I help them understand what it is about and then get on with life?"

Paul wrote in Ephesians 5:21, "Submit to one another out of reverence for Christ" (NIV). I believe this verse applies to sharing the pain. We cannot keep reliving it, but we need to own each other's pain through submission. Scripture also says, "Bear one another's burdens, and so fulfill the law of Christ" (Gal. 6:2).

When we own each other's pain, we share the joy that comes from going through difficult situations together yet emerging victorious.

Understanding the pain comes from recognizing the pain God feels because of mankind. God owned pain for mankind when He saw Satan had corrupted their minds.

Adam and Eve reacted negatively toward their Creator in the garden. They hid from Him when He called. God knew that His fellowship and trust with man had been broken. God experienced pain as He put Adam and Eve out of the garden of Eden. A part of being reconciled to God through Jesus Christ is recognizing the pain mankind brought to God through our betrayal.

African Americans, Japanese Americans, Hispanic Americans, Native Americans and others who have been hurt deeply by other races can share the joy and the faith that has come in their lives from these shared experiences. They've gained a whole new tenacity and strength in their lives. White Americans can share their wealth and resources. Everyone must share.

I believe that is why God has created this pain as a part of our experience. It not only gives a vision of a holy life but also a passion for a holy life. People who have reached a low point emerge stronger and more passionate. We must have that same passion. People who have not dipped to this low depression can learn from those who have been there. Through the shared experiences we become stronger in our relationships.

When men come together in a Promise Keepers event, they share these types of relational experiences. They are able to talk with each other as brothers and share across racial and denominational lines. The walls come down as they interact.

How to Get Started

How do you begin the process when you come face-to-face with the need for racial reconciliation? You begin as the Holy Spirit moves you to share the pain.

Sometimes pain is only brought out as you come face-to-face with people who have pain directed at you. We must respond to the pain and choose not to ignore it.

Whether we want to acknowledge it or not, through the years the world is increasingly becoming an institution of non-Caucasian peoples. What will happen as we come into more contact with people from different races? Before you can respond to them, you must realize the pain. Then can you begin the ministry of reconciliation.

POINTS TO PONDER

1. In the opening pages of this chapter, I gave you an example about sharing pain during the process of reconciliation. Consider the cost of reconciliation and the pain you will face. Make a decision about how you will handle this pain.

2. Reconciliation will mean initiating conversations with people of other races about their past experiences. Some of these decisions will involve honing your listening skills, lowering your defenses and developing transparency and honesty. Make sure you're ready for each decision.

   ✓ Evaluate ahead of time how you will initiate and then carry out these conversations.

3. I point to the life of Zacchaeus in the New Testament as someone ready to admit his failures from the past. Consider your past and your failures.

   ✓ Reread the story of Zacchaeus in Luke 19. What clues can you take from the life of Zacchaeus?

4. Note that Jesus didn't make a popular decision when He visited with Zacchaeus. Sometimes in the movement of reconciliation you will need to go against the crowd.

✓ Consider the unpopular nature of breaking down the walls in your own life. Who do you think may oppose your resolve?

✓ What steps in the process of reconciliation will you need to take to minister to the whole person?

✓ Will you get involved financially or socially or some other way?

✓ You will need to go through the steps of purification as discussed in 1 Peter 1:22. How will this verse be applied to your life as you tear down the walls?

6. Return to the story of my special friendship with Gordon England. Sharing my painful story about integration with Gordon took effort for both of us. Maybe you will carry the role that I had and become more vulnerable and willing to talk about this subject with people of other races. Or possibly you will have to take the role that Gordon filled — patiently yet persistently pursuing an understanding of the pain.

✓ Evaluate your current walk on the topic of reconciliation and determine which role you will need to take to encourage tearing down the walls.

7. Coach Bill McCartney has said about

reconciliation, "There is no war without causalities."

✓ What are the possible ramifications and costs you will face in your own journey to tear down the walls?

✓ What can you learn from the role model of Bill McCartney?

CHAPTER 5

THE MINISTRY OF RECONCILIATION

A prominent leader in the Christian community called me with tears in his voice. "Brother Phil, I called you to ask your help. This is very confidential. I don't know what to do. I've been going to meetings with this group of pastors who are predominately African American. But I don't think I can keep doing it."

After a pause this brother continued to tell me his story. "Every time I go I'm either the only Anglo or one of the few Anglos in attendance. When I'm there I'm always put down, reviled or castigated in some way — not only me but leaders of other organizations who are attempting to do good. I don't understand it. Why is it always about politics? Brother Phil, I thought it was just about us loving each other."

I heard the pain in this brother's voice. And I said, "I'm sure glad we're friends, brother, and we respect each other and have a long-standing relationship. You're right. Everything needs to be based on love. But politics and economics do come into this. In order to meet spiritual needs you have to meet felt needs — whether hunger or housing or crime. Until their felt needs are met it is hard to get through to the deeper spiritual problems."

As Jesus ministered to people He recognized there were times He needed to minister to the physical needs of the people as well as the spiritual. Matthew 15:32-37 records:

> Now Jesus called His disciples to Himself and said, "I have compassion on the multitude...I do not want to send them away hungry, lest they faint on the way."
>
> Then His disciples said to Him, "Where could we get enough bread in the wilderness to fill such a great multitude?"
>
> Jesus said to them, "How many loaves do you have?"
>
> And they said, "Seven, and a few little fish."
>
> He took the seven loaves and the fish and gave thanks, broke them and gave

them to His disciples; and the disciples gave to the multitude. So they all ate and were filled.

Jesus took time to minister to their felt needs. We must do no less than the example of Jesus.

This white brother continued talking with me. "I called you, Brother Phil, because we worked together in another group where the going got rough. We shared that pain as only a few people could do. We didn't give up on our relationship because of the pain."

I agreed with this friend. "Yes, you never win by giving up. When you have a mandate from the Lord you need to be willing to sacrifice, just like the Lord sacrificed Himself. If you can sacrifice your pride and self-worth then the Lord can continue to use you in this group."

This brother and I prayed together on the phone, and I promised the next time I was in his city I would join him at one of the meetings.

In the movement of racial reconciliation we shouldn't leave people alone to struggle. We should come alongside them in the struggle. The Lord Jesus didn't leave us alone on the earth but sent the Holy Spirit to comfort us.

THE HEART OF GOD IS RECONCILIATION

Reconciliation goes beyond the law of the land or personal experiences. Reconciliation is in the heart of God.

A Jewish man named Nicodemus came to Jesus in

the middle of the night. Jesus told this religious leader that he must be born again. Then Jesus talked about reconciliation. In one of the most quoted passages of Scripture He said:

> For God so loved the world that He gave His only begotten Son, that whoever believes in Him should not perish but have everlasting life. For God did not send His Son into the world to condemn the world, but that the world through Him might be saved (John 3:16-17).

God loves us so much that He wants everyone to be reconciled to Him and the Lord Jesus. The Creator of the universe doesn't want anyone to perish but desires everyone to have eternal life.

Because of our relationship with God through Jesus Christ, He has given each of us the ministry of reconciliation. Second Corinthians 5:17-19 says:

> Therefore, if anyone is in Christ, he is a new creation; old things have passed away; behold, all things have become new. Now all things are of God, who has reconciled us to Himself through Jesus Christ, and has given us the *ministry of reconciliation,* that is, that God was in Christ reconciling the world to Himself, not imputing their trespasses to them, and has committed to us the word of reconciliation (italics added).

Through Jesus Christ we have gained a new connection to the Lord of the universe.

There is a story told about when Jesus returned to heaven. One angel asked Jesus, "How is it that You've returned so soon from the earth?"

Jesus said with a smile, "My work was finished."

The angel shook his head with astonishment and said, "Finished? It seemed as though You had only begun Your work. To whom then did You leave the work?"

Jesus told the angel that He left the work in the hands of the chosen disciples. Jesus had committed His life and teaching to these twelve men. The angel looked surprised and said, "To that motley crew?"

And Jesus said, "Yes."

"Well, what happens if they fail?" the angel continued to push.

Jesus said, "If they fail, then the work won't get done."

Of course we know that the disciples didn't fail. The Father promised these disciples that another Comforter would come and abide with them. The Holy Spirit empowered their lives to carry on the work of Jesus. That same Holy Spirit can reign in our hearts and lives today.

If we are to carry out the work of racial reconciliation, we must first believe the promise of the Father — that He will come and abide with us. He will be in us as we pray, wait on Him and seek His presence in our lives. When Father God takes complete control of our lives, then we can have relationships that aren't in our own strength and energy. These new relationships will be in the energy of the Holy Spirit. As Jesus is the Lord of our lives, He can take control.

After this happens we are empowered by the Holy Spirit to carry out the life-changing, life-giving, life-sustaining work of reconciliation.

Lessons From the Walls of Jericho

After wandering in the wilderness for forty years the children of Israel were ready to conquer the promised land. Yet when they reached the city of Jericho, they were confronted with walls. These high structures stood between them and the promises of God. The walls in Jericho were massive with great height and durability and strength. While these were physical walls, the force that brought them down was a spiritual force.

Joshua told the children of Israel about the commands of God. The people chose to obey God and march in cadence around the walls of this great city. As they marched, the people got into step with the will of God. Every day, once a day, they marched around the walls. On the seventh day they marched seven times in a single day. That's when those massive walls came tumbling down (Josh. 6:20).

Marching around the walls of Jericho wasn't easy. Imagine the nation of Israel. The people had to get up every day — on time — and march in step with each other. These people didn't have the same temperament, ability, vision and passion. But they were obedient to the call of God.

Each morning for six days they were up at the appropriate time and walked in step with each other around those walls. As they listened to God's voice for the seventh time on the seventh day, the walls came crashing down and they conquered the city.

This story can teach us about the walls that are built up against reconciliation. To break down these spiritual walls in our relationships and bring harmony to the races, denominations and people, the first step is to be in tune with God. As we listen to God's voice in our lives we will be sensitive to others and will be able to reach across these walls. As with Jericho it won't be easy, but when God is involved the walls will fall.

THE WORTH OF THE INDIVIDUAL

By God's grace and design I've been groomed to work in this area of racial reconciliation. It's not that I'm a banner-carrying crusader. I'm not a loud-talking, glad-hander kind of guy in this area. But I've always been willing to reach across racial barriers.

When Dr. Lloyd Ogilvie, former pastor for Hollywood Presbyterian Church and now the sixty-first chaplain of the United States Senate, asked me if I would open a senate session in prayer, I said yes. That's the same answer I gave to Dr. Howard Hendricks of Dallas Theological Seminary, Dr. John Maxwell and Pastor Jack Hayford. I've been willing to share with these people as people — not as an African American talking with a white person. In the midst of our conversations I'm always conscious of their color and appreciative of their contributions, but it doesn't make a difference in my actions.

The reconciler and person who would let the

walls fall down is a lover of people as people. He sees the worth of every individual and at the same time he realizes that every person has failures and successes. When we see our interdependence, then we become willing to admit our failures. When Jesus is present in your life you bring about that transformation.

The apostle Paul wrote:

> I beseech you therefore, brethren, by the mercies of God, that you present your bodies a living sacrifice, holy, acceptable to God, which is your reasonable service. And do not be conformed to this world, but be transformed by the renewing of your mind, that you may prove what is that good and acceptable and perfect will of God (Rom. 12:1-2).

The process of becoming a reconciler doesn't happen overnight. It takes offering our lives daily to God. Then as we offer our lives to God we are fitted to His pattern for our lives — not our own methods but God's methods. Then we are transformed into the people of God. As believers and people of God, we can relate to people as people — not because they are a certain race or color.

MIMICKING OR COMMITMENT

During my junior year of college the racial integration policies changed, and restaurants had opened so African Americans and whites could eat in the same place and come through the same doors.

For a number of years I had worked at a restaurant as a fry cook. Once I decided to go out with a number of my white friends to the restaurant so we could eat lunch. Being college kids, we ate practically everything in sight and had a wonderful time. We racked up a pretty good bill.

When the waiter brought the bill and laid it down, everyone made the usual comments, then one guy said, "I'll pay that bill."

Someone else said, "No, I'll pay it."

Two other guys chimed in, "I'll pay it." Finally, because it seemed like the thing do, I chimed in. I decided it would be rude not to offer to pay for the bill.

The minute I offered to pay the others responded almost in unison, "OK, let Phil pay it." This group had contrived ahead of time for me to pay the bill. They figured that since this was the restaurant where I had worked I could pick up the bill, no matter how big it was.

I was shocked that they agreed to my offer. Everybody got up from the table laughing about how Phil was going to pay the bill. I paid that big bill which I was not prepared to pay.

This story is a lesson about what happens when you mimic without commitment in the area of reconciliation. You get stuck with a bill which you aren't prepared to pay. When you are committed, then you are not just mouthing something, but you are prepared to pay the bill — whether it is pain or martyrdom — you are ready.

On this particular occasion I was not ready for

the cost. Because I was stuck with it from mimicking, it left a bitter taste in my mouth. I never went out to eat with those guys again.

You can flirt with racial reconciliation, but are you committed to doing something about it?

THE IMPORTANCE OF RELATIONSHIPS

The importance of these relationships transcends the racial barrier. When I was pastoring a church part-time I was also cooking at The White Spot in Denver. One of my regular customers was Sid Cellars. This rancher and oilman often came into the restaurant with his daughter. Sid liked his steak and eggs cooked in a special way, and I delighted to fix them for him.

We developed a real friendship and admiration for each other. We talked about a lot of things when we were together. I told him about my plans to be a full-time pastor someday. Sid said, "Well, if you ever need anything, let me know." I couldn't think of anything pressing at the moment, so I tucked the invitation away. It would come in handy another day.

In 1966 we rented a building for our meetings, and suddenly the building was sold. We looked for another building for our fledgling congregation. One day we found an old piece of property that was for sale. There was one difficulty. As estate property the lot had to be sold for $3,400 and had to be paid in full and not carried on a loan. I needed something quick for my congregation, but I didn't have any money.

My wife and I both got paid on the same day. We

went to see the landlord for this property and made an offer. "Just take this as a down payment, and then we'll pay the rest in payments," I offered.

"What?" he said. "I told you that this was estate property and had to be sold outright."

I said, "You know, the Lord told me to get this piece of property, and He also told me to give you a plan." I thought I had a new idea back then in 1966. "I'll give you this one thousand dollars, and then I'll pay the rest of it in three payments. And if we miss any payment, then we will forfeit the entire amount."

He laughed and told me, "Young man, I hope you know what you are doing." We signed a note that spelled out the payment schedule and the terms. He took my one thousand dollars as a down payment. As I went out the door he reminded me, "If you can't make the payment it's your own fault. You came up with this idea on your own."

"Oh, no," I assured him. "We can do it."

We paid the first thousand then we made the other two payments. When it came time for the final thousand-dollar payment I knew I wasn't going to have the money by the specified date.

Before it was due I went to see the real estate agent responsible for the property. "I'm a week early to see you," I told him, "but it looks like I won't have the money on time. I want you to give me a few more weeks. I've been good on all the other payments."

He broke out laughing, "You told me that God told you. You tell God that He'd better get that money because if you don't, you've lost everything."

I was shaken from his laughter and unwillingness to extend the time limit. I began to walk down Broadway Street. I had no idea where I was going. As I walked I prayed for a solution to this situation. At about 13th and Broadway, the Lord brought to mind Sid Cellars, who worked in a nearby office complex.

I had no idea what to ask Sid. Should I ask him to loan me one thousand dollars or what? I was directed there so I went. When I walked into his office Sid greeted me, "Phillip Porter, how are you doing, young man? Have a seat." So I sat down.

We chatted for a few minutes, then I said, "I'm here because I have a real problem, and I don't know how to deal with it. I need your advice." I told him the story about the agreement and the purchase of the property.

"You mean to tell me you paid that guy all but one thousand dollars, and you weren't behind on any payments?" Sid asked.

"That's correct," I said.

Then he asked me to repeat the name of the real estate agent, which I did.

"Give me that phone there," Sid said. He picked up the phone and called the agent. Evidently they were old friends, and I sat listening to them chat back and forth.

Then Sid said, "Hey, I've got a young man here named Porter who tells me a fantastic story. He says that he owes you one thousand dollars, and you won't give him any credit."

On the other end of the phone the agent must have been laughing. But Sid continued the conversation,

"You can cut the laughter because you're going to give this young man some time to pay this note. I could loan Porter the one thousand dollars and give it to you, but I'm not going to do that. You owe me, and I'm calling in one of my favors. I want you to give him a year to pay that one thousand dollars off."

Sid hung up the phone and said, "You go on back there, Porter. If you've any more trouble then you get on back to me."

When I walked into the agent's office he was fuming. He said, "You had this concocted all of the time. You knew what you were going to do. You knew that guy, and I have to do what he says." To this day I have no idea what power Sid Cellars had over that man, but whatever it was he wrote me an agreement that gave me a year to pay off the thousand dollars.

This blessing came from the fruits of a relationship. Both of these men were white businessmen, and here I was a young, twenty-something, black church man. I was just a cook at The White Spot, but I took advantage of that position to make friends.

We built a relationship across racial lines to accomplish what needed to be done. I only needed Sid that one time, but he sure came through for me in a fantastic way.

POINTS TO PONDER

1. Return to the story where my white friend was attending the pastor's meeting. Can you feel the pain of his struggle with reconciliation?

    ✓ How can you apply the principle, "You never win by giving up?"

2. Reconciliation will not be easy. Revisit the story of the children of Israel walking around the high walls of Jericho.

    ✓ What characteristics about their success can you apply in your life? Do you need their persistence, their obedience to God, their ear to listen to God? Ask the Holy Spirit to shine a light into your life and show you where you need to grow.

3. I told a story which illustrates a clear-cut difference between mimicking and commitment. In Revelation 3:15-16, we see how God feels about commitment. Take time to read this passage and decide whether you are going to be "cold or hot."

    ✓ Are you toying with the idea of breaking down the walls, or are you committed?

    ✓ Which way are you headed with reconciliation?

4. A key principle in reconciliation is the importance of relationships. If we have the courage to build relationships across racial, denominational and other boundaries, they often transcend other difficulties or barriers.

✓ How can you apply my lesson on relationship with Sid Cellars to your own friendships and relationships?

CHAPTER 6

IT BEGINS
IN THE HEART

In 1962 I became a part of the Colorado Civil Rights Commission. We had a mixed race staff. Our job was to investigate complaints of civil rights violations regarding housing, employment and public accommodation.

There was an influx of laws regarding civil rights. As our commission listened to complaints and investigated violations, I quickly learned that it was the heart of man that needed changing. Such changes wouldn't come from legislation. A famous civil rights leader said, "Though it makes me feel good to know I can walk through the Southern states and not be lynched at will, I would feel better if I knew these men loved me."

WHEN THE HEART DOESN'T CHANGE

At a well-known and respected Denver company I investigated a discrimination situation and made an appointment to meet with the president. He got right to the point. "Young man, you don't need to come to me with all your data. We know that we discriminate." Then after a pause he continued, "But we know how to discriminate. You get your boss and bring him to me, then we can talk and work this thing out. Good day."

I was dismissed from the conversation as the man turned to the paperwork on his desk. This company president knew he could work out something with the director of the commission due to his contacts. After several other similar incidents I realized the only way to change men was to change their hearts.

I walked away from that situation with some major questions about the future direction of my life. Because I wanted to pastor a church since very early in my life, at first I declared my major to be theology and Bible. This way I could have a good basis for my pastorate. Then I got cold feet. I didn't believe that my little church in my denomination would be able to afford someone to work as a full-time pastor. I changed my major to sociology and kept my minor in Bible.

My dad was my role model for ministry. Throughout his life my dad divided his work between two paths — ministry and secular work. He had a small Church of God in Christ congregation. He also traveled around the smaller towns nearby Enid, Oklahoma, as a pastor. These congregations didn't have the resources to hire a full-time pastor so my dad served in this capacity.

My dad had a deep love and affection for his work for the Lord. He built new churches or worked on remodeling existing buildings so they could be used as churches. His work with people gave him a great deal of pleasure and satisfaction. But beyond the work of the church, Dad had to support his wife and ten children. He was a tent-maker, a person working at a trade to earn a living while ministering in his free time. Though often working several jobs at the same time, Dad provided for his family.

From observing my father I followed along the dual paths of a pastor and a social worker. We started a little church in a west Denver community in 1963. At the same time I worked at the civil rights commission, wanting to be active in social change through the laws of the land.

When that company president told me, "We know how to discriminate," I reached my decision point. I decided that in order to preach the gospel effectively I needed to live by the gospel and make that my central focus. For at least four years the fact that I tried to reach people for the gospel while maintaining my position in the secular workforce gnawed at me. My father had done the same thing, more out of necessity to provide for his family, but I wanted something different.

Discrimination is not a matter of laws, but it is a matter of the heart. Men's hearts need to change. I decided, "Lord, I need to begin with myself. I'm ready to go into full-time pastoral ministry." I decided to touch hearts where I was — in the western Denver community. While I had passion for this type of ministry, I was unsure how the Lord would bring it about. The first step was my own availability.

Only a few months earlier I had wrestled with this decision in my prayers. Now Lee and I had six children, and a seventh child would arrive in a few months. We attended the annual holy convocation in Memphis, Tennessee. We stayed in a small home on Boxtown Road. During one of the evenings at the convocation I agonized over my decision. How in the world was I going to support my wife and family on what the church paid me — $348 per month? My pay from the Civil Rights Commission was a little over one thousand dollars per month. How would we make it? I knew my faith would rest in the almighty God, but my faith didn't seem strong.

The private home where we stayed was in a swamp area near a thick forest of trees. One night I was awakened by a dream. A choir of angels was singing. In the background I could hear the crickets, and it was as if they were an orchestra for the angels, who were singing:

> Is your all on the altar of sacrifice laid?
> Your heart does the Spirit control?
> You can only be blest

And have peace and sweet rest
As you yield Him your body and soul.

The angels were singing this chorus of a hymn that we sang in churches at the time. I shook my wife. She woke up, gave me some more of the lyrics and went back to sleep.

Throughout the night I laid there half asleep and half awake. The song was playing through my mind. It came as an affirmation and a challenge to me. I needed to trust the Lord and go into full-time ministry.

We came home after the meeting. About a week before Christmas I gathered my family together in our living room. I told them what the Lord had laid on my heart about going into full-time ministry.

My announcement caught my wife by surprise. She said, "Oh, honey. Are you sure? We're just starting to get somewhere with our lives and have something for our children. We don't even have health or accident insurance."

My wife and I married during my second year of college. She helped to put me through school. Now we were ten years out of college, and I had finally landed a good job with the Civil Rights Commission following six years in the restaurant business. We had escalated our lifestyle and purchased a second and larger home. Life was much better.

I looked my wife in the eye and said, "I'm working for God now. He's going to provide the health and accident insurance." She raised several other questions, but I reassured my family that where God guides He provides.

I asked them, "Haven't I provided for you up

until now? Then trust me and trust God."

My wife said, "I'm in your corner, Phil. I've never been a hindrance to you."

In January 1970 I resigned my position with the Colorado Civil Rights Commission. Although my congregation at the time was small, less than fifty members, we launched into full-time ministry with the idea to touch the entire city of Denver and change the hearts of men. Yet I needed to pay the bills for my family. I kicked my ministry into high gear with a vengeance. I held revivals and early morning prayer meetings in addition to my church work. The first three years were an intense struggle.

Somewhere in the back of my mind I think I had decided to give God three years to see what He would do. I had many doubts and second thoughts. Over those three years things had gotten materially worse, but spiritually they had improved greatly. I was more mature and challenged.

Yet my bills were mounting, and my concern was great. One morning in prayer I told God, "I've given You three years. Lord, this thing isn't coming together. I'm still young enough to get back into secular work and make a living. I'm strongly considering this possibility, Lord."

I remember the Lord speaking to my spirit and saying, "How could you give Me what you don't have? You haven't given Me any three years. Instead, you've been trying to challenge Me for three years. You can't challenge Me. Either you believe Me and trust Me or you might as well return to your work. You'll be safe at your secular job. And when you decide to retire you'll have a nice little congregation. You can go from there if that is what you want, or you can decide to trust Me completely and see what I'll do."

I prayed, "Oh, Lord, there is no question about it. I want to trust You completely." Now the driving force for my life was to deal with what God said to me. I prayed, "God, I'm here, and I've not touched the heart of this city. How do I do it?" I started to pray, fast and wait before God. Bit by bit the Lord revealed His plan.

One day the Lord spoke in my spirit and said, "What is it that I've given you that you could use to touch the city?" Such a prodding disturbed me. I wasn't sure of the answer, but the continual prodding of the Spirit made me search.

I said, "Lord, I love speaking."

"Right," the Lord said, "I've given that to you." Then there was more prodding from the Lord. "What else have I given you?" I thought about how much I love people.

"Right," the Lord said. "And what spiritual gift have I given you?"

I remember telling the Lord that it was prayer. It was the greatest gift that I had, and my preaching didn't compare to that.

"Right," the Lord said. "Now take those three gifts and put them together." For hours I wondered how I could put them together. Finally I got an idea — broadcasting. We didn't have any money to go on television, but radio was less expensive.

I went to the local radio station, KQXI, where I had already been hosting a live program on Saturdays and Sundays for the past three years. I presented them with a new concept: Each day I would come into the studio and open the telephone lines. People could call in with prayer requests, and I would minister to them with prayer.

The words Jesus told His disciples became my opening on the radio:

> Assuredly, I say to you, whatever you bind on earth will be bound in heaven, and whatever you loose on earth will be loosed in heaven. For where two or three are gathered together in My name, I am there in the midst of them (Matt. 18:19-20).

Even today I continue to hear about the fruit from my daily prayers on that radio program. It was called *It's Prayer Time* and ran from 9 A.M. until 9:15 A.M. six days a week. *It's Prayer Time* started in November 1973 and lasted until 1991. It became the longest running daily prayer ministry in this entire Rocky Mountain region.

Rick Kingham, now the vice president of field ministries at Promise Keepers, recently told about how the program touched his heart. During a time for leadership appreciation, Rick told the group, "Twenty years ago when I came to Denver from Rockwall, Texas, I came from a church that was strong in prayer. One day while tuning the radio, I heard this gravelly voice say, "It's prayer time.""

Rick said he thought, *What is this that radio waves would be used for prayer ministry?* It was a new twist on prayer for this young man. He told the group of men, "For over twenty years, Bishop Porter has provided leadership and blessing for the city of Denver. Now he's our leader here at Promise Keepers and our man of choice."

We were able to be a blessing to many people and their congregations because we came alongside people as their prayer partners on a daily basis. The prayer ministry crossed different denominations and races. I put together my three gifts, and God touched the hearts of a city and its people.

CHANGED TO REFLECT THE HEART OF GOD

Through *It's Prayer Time* we changed peoples' hearts, and they began to seek the heart of God. The heart of God is for reconciliation and unity. It conforms us to Christ's prayer in John 17:22, "that they may be one just as We are one."

The heart, which is the center of human activity, has always been of particular interest to God. In the Old Testament God spoke through the prophet Jeremiah, "And I will give you shepherds according to My heart, who will feed you with knowledge and understanding" (Jer. 3:15).

The prophet Samuel said to King Saul regarding David, "The Lord has sought for Himself a man after His own heart" (1 Sam. 13:14). In Psalm 51:10 David said, "Create in me a clean heart, O God, and renew a steadfast spirit within me." We're told not only to love the Lord with our strength and mind but with our whole heart (Mark 12:30).

David was so committed to God that he wanted to bring the ark of the covenant back to Israel. He knew the ark represented the heart of God. Inside the ark was a jar of manna, the rod of Aaron which had blossomed and the commandments of God written on stone. Whenever the ark was present, it signified the divine presence of God in their midst. The ark had been stolen, and David wanted to get it back for the people. So he approached the people with his heart's desire.

We can learn a key lesson from David's actions. When your heart is committed to God, then you stir others and changes come about.

David spoke to the people about the ark and wanting it returned to Jerusalem. As the people transported the ark, they ignored God's instructions. According to the laws of God no one was to touch the ark of the covenant. The priests were to put the ark on poles and carry the poles on their shoulders. Instead the people put the ark on a cart and had a pair of oxen pull it.

At one point the ark began to fall off the cart, and Uzzah reached out to touch it and keep it from falling. At that touch God immediately killed Uzzah (2 Sam. 6:1-7). Because of Uzzah's death, David decided to leave the ark at the house of Obed-Edom (v. 10).

This story points out another principle for touching the heart of God. As we approach God we have to come to Him in His manner and with purity. We must follow the Lord's commandments and directions at all costs so we will be blessed. Over and over, the people in the Bible proved that following God was the way of success.

When the ark of the covenant was left at the house of Obed-Edom, that family gained a blessing from God. King David observed the blessing of God on Obed-Edom's house and decided to move the ark on into Jerusalem.

"Where the Spirit of the Lord is, there is liberty," says 2 Corinthians 3:17. Now with the right relationship of his heart, David returned and got the **ark of the covenant.** As David brought the ark into Jerusalem, his heart broke out into tremendous praise and rejoicing. The soldiers rejoiced with David as he danced before the ark while the people looked on.

God moves in one heart at a time, but where there is a contagious attitude of joy and devotion to God, one man can change a nation. The life of David shows us this type of action.

From one man sin entered the world, and also by one man, the Lord Jesus, mankind escaped death from sin. One man, Christ Jesus, provides righteousness to everyone (Rom. 5:18). Through Jesus, reconciliation and tearing down the walls between people, races and denominations becomes contagious.

WHERE THE HEART CHANGES

During my years in Denver I've observed numerous experiences in which people changed their hearts. Through *It's Prayer Time* people called with their requests, and one woman in particular called frequently. She began with, "How are you this glorious morning?" She had a wonderful Southern accent and became almost a trademark of my radio program. One day she invited me to her home in Aurora. My wife and I went to visit her.

We met Sally*, who grew up in a preacher's home. She was a white woman and a bit surprised that I was black.

We had a wonderful time together. Then she said, "My dad's going to come out for a visit, and I want him to listen to you and fall in love with your program as I have done," Sally said with a smile. "My dad is elderly, and I want him to give you his library when he passes away."

Before long the father came to visit and called into the program. He commended me for my program. Sally extended another invitation for us to visit her home. She explained, "My father has always been prejudiced and taught us to be prejudiced. I want him to meet you."

When we walked in the door her father was awestruck. He never expected I would be black. This kind, retired minister and I had a good conversation together. I prayed for him because he was sick.

A few months later he died and left me about sixty books from his library with a note. In part he said, "Because you prayed for me and because I know the effect your program and ministry had on my wayward daughter's life I've changed my attitude, and I leave these books with you." He explained that the bulk of his library had already been promised to his alma mater. I was thrilled with this concrete evidence of a changed heart.

Another example of a changed heart came in 1977. Our church was growing, and we sought a larger facility. We were ten thousand dollars short of what we needed to purchase a piece of property.

*Names have been changed for the privacy of those involved.

The church board wouldn't allow us to borrow this money. I was in my study praying before I went on the radio program one day and received a phone call.

A man named Dan was calling. "My wife Jill and I are rejoicing that we have had one year of joy in our marriage after calling your program for prayer." I rejoiced with this man over his good news. Then he continued, "As we were thinking about you, the Lord laid you on our hearts. We're not wealthy and we have several children. We can't give you any money, but we do have a small amount that you could borrow without interest for a year."

I expressed my appreciation for the offer. Maybe this was the answer for our shortage of funds. *Even if it was one thousand dollars it would help us,* I thought.

"It's only ten thousand dollars," Dan said. It was exactly what we needed for the land! This white Catholic man became one of my soul brothers as we worked together for the cause of Christ. This experience was simply another example of the love of Jesus reaching beyond racial walls and barriers.

Biblical Evidences of a Changed Heart

In many different passages of the Bible we learn about people whose hearts have been changed. In the Old Testament, the Queen of Sheba heard about Solomon and his wisdom. The queen decided that she needed to do more than hear about the wisdom of Solomon. She needed to experience it firsthand. So she traveled from her home in Ethiopia to Jerusalem. When she arrived in Jerusalem, the queen tested

Solomon with hard questions. He answered all of her questions, and she saw the evidence of his wisdom. The experience changed her forever (2 Chr. 9:1-9).

We may not need to experience segregation and the barriers of race in order to change our hearts and tear down the walls. When Jesus Christ comes into our lives in a full way, Jesus sees us, sizes us up, reads us the record of our past sins and then gives us hope.

Jesus changed people's hearts. One of the greatest evidences of changed hearts was Simon Peter. When Andrew brought his brother to Jesus, the Messiah said, "You are Simon the son of Jonah. You shall be called Cephas" (John 1:42).

In essence Jesus told this disciple, "I know who you are. I know your pedigree and background. In fact, I know your daddy." (Fathers are always significant in the lives of their offspring.) "He's a fisherman and owns a big boat down there. You have that company named 'Jonah and Sons.' And you're the brother with the big mouth. I know you. Even so, you've come and I'm going to make you a fisher of men." Jesus didn't beat around the bush and ignore the topic.

Today we're bound up in denominational and racial barriers. But Jesus can cut right to the heart of the matter.

When Jesus entered Simon Peter's house, he brought about change. Let's think about this question: How does Jesus bring about change when He enters a house?

Jesus always makes an impact when He enters a house. In Matthew 2:11, after Jesus' birth in the stable transformed it into a place of divine worship. A lowly stable was so changed that wise men came from the east to visit it. When these men of great learning and importance walked into the stable, they knelt down and worshiped Him. Then they opened their treasures and presented gifts to Jesus — gold, frankincense and myrrh (Matt. 2:11). Jesus changed a simple stable into a place of worship by His presence in the house.

Remember the story of Zacchaeus that we talked about earlier? Zacchaeus was a dishonest, sinful man. But when Jesus came to his house Zacchaeus changed. He promised to repay the people he had cheated. No longer would his home be a source of contempt to his neighbors. It would be a home ruled by the compassion of Christ.

When Jesus came into the house of Simon Peter and Andrew, Peter's mother-in-law was sick with a fever. "So He came and took her by the hand and lifted her up, and immediately the fever left her. And she served them" (Mark 1:31). Jesus came into this house of sickness, and by His healing touch He changed the atmosphere and mood of the house.

A feeling of prejudice and sickness may be in your house today. It may weigh on you because of a broken relationship in your home or a strained relationship at work. Possibly it is across denominational lines or racial lines. When Jesus enters our lives we are changed into people God directs and uses. The apostle Paul wrote about how our bodies are the temples of the Holy Spirit. When we give our lives to God, He can change us — but only if Jesus is in the house.

Later Jesus brought His changing power to a house in Capernaum. The crowds had packed the home to hear Jesus. Two friends brought a paralytic but couldn't get him in through the door or a window. So they carried their friend onto the roof of the house. *If only Jesus will see our friend, then he will be changed,* they thought. First they ripped into the ceiling of the house and removed parts of the roof. Then with ropes they lowered the paralyzed man down to Jesus (Luke 5:17-19).

Jesus draws people to Him for healing or a blessing or to relieve whatever need a person has.

As Jesus traveled around Israel, He went to the house of Mary and Martha. This story shows the contrasting responses people have to Jesus. Mary sat at the foot of Jesus to listen to His teaching and learn from His tremendous wisdom and understanding. She was awed and blessed by the Lord.

Martha was busy with many details of the household and food preparation. Martha went to Jesus and said, "Lord, do You not care that my sister has left me to serve alone? Therefore tell her to help me" (Luke 10:40).

Then Jesus said to her, "Martha, Martha, you are worried and troubled about many things. But one thing is needed, and Mary has chosen that good part, which will not be taken away from her" (vv. 41-42).

Finally in Revelation 3:20-21, Jesus says:

> Behold, I stand at the door and knock. If anyone hears My voice and opens the door, I will come in to him and dine with

him, and he with Me. To him who over-
comes I will grant to sit with Me on My
throne, as I also overcame and sat down
with My Father on His throne

Jesus wants to enter your house to make a difference in your life.

Since we have been created in God's image and
likeness, our hearts and bodies were designed to
house the love, grace and fellowship of God. Sin
entered, brokenness came, bitterness took root and
we wandered away from God and became distant
from each other.

Reconciliation is God's work which brings us
back into right relationships with Him and others.
As we give up control of our lives to God, then
Jesus can enter the house and transform it. Through
His strength and energy we can break down the
walls of prejudice in our lives.

POINTS TO PONDER

1. Instead of social change through civil rights I decided that reconciliation would only come from changed hearts.

   ✓ Have you come face-to-face with people not interested in change?

   ✓ How did you deal with these people?

   Recount several of your experiences to a friend or someone in your study group.

2. I decided that a changed heart needed to begin with myself. I stepped out in faith into full-time ministry. The Spirit of God leads each of us differently. You may be called to continue working in corporate America or God may be leading your heart in another direction.

   ✓ How can you increase your sensitivity to God's leading and direction?

   Possibly you need to commit more time to prayer or study of God's Word. What each person needs to do will be different.

   ✓ Write down your need, then plot out a strategy for growth in this area.

3. *It's Prayer Time* brought together people from all races and denominations under a single focused goal — prayer.

   ✓ How can you take steps to break

down the walls in your life through prayer?

4. Prayer is a way we can merge our desires and our plans with God's desires and plans for us.

   ✓ Take focused time this coming week and spend it in prayer. Beyond asking God for your requests, spend time listening to God's voice then following His direction.

5. Take some time to read in 2 Samuel about the life of David, a man after God's own heart. David's life wasn't perfect. He failed, yet he continually sought a relationship with his heavenly Father.

   ✓ What encouragement and strength can you gain from studying the life of David?

6. Sometimes as we change, people around us also open up to the ideas of reconciliation. Consider the ripple effect in the story of Sally when she called *It's Prayer Time*. Sally returned to a personal relationship with Christ, and her father became a little less prejudiced.

   ✓ Take a few minutes to dream about what will happen as you tear down the walls in your own life and move toward reconciliation.

✓ Speculate about the ripple effect in your home or friends; then pray and ask God to make it happen.

7. I listed a number of examples from the Bible about what happens when Jesus is in the house.

✓ Reflect on these Bible stories.

✓ What actions do you need to take so that Jesus has a stronger presence in your life and home?

✓ Plan some concrete steps of growth to take during the next week.

CHAPTER 7

FIVE STEPS TO TEARING DOWN THE WALLS

I've compressed the process of tearing down the walls into five steps. Imagine a wall with five rows of bricks. Each row represents a step in the process of breaking down the wall. With each step you take down a row of bricks in your walled relationships.

The top row of bricks in the wall is torn down through *compassion*. As Jesus comes into our lives and fills our hearts with His presence, we are also filled with His compassion for people.

Throughout the Gospels Jesus shows compassion for people (see Matt. 9:36; 14:14; 20:34; Mark 1:41; 5:19; and Luke 7:13). In Matthew 20, two blind men called out to Jesus as He was walking by. They begged Him to have mercy on them and asked Him to open their eyes.

> So Jesus had compassion and touched their eyes. And immediately their eyes received sight, and they followed Him (v. 34).

Jesus was so full of compassion that He desired to heal these blind men. In the same way, His compassion within us moves us to take action in correcting a wrong in someone's life.

In terms of reconciliation, these wrongs may be discrimination and prejudice a person has suffered because of his race or denomination. Compassion moves us to reach out to others and bring healing to these wounds. Only after we build our relationship with Jesus and learn of His love can we begin to tear down the first layer of the walls in other relationships.

The second level of bricks can be removed through *consideration*. After our hearts are softened and compassionate about reconciliation, we need to go to the other person and listen to their response. Listening to the response isn't easy.

In chapter 4 I wrote about how we need to feel the pain of the other person. It takes consideration for us to ask about and then listen to that pain. The words may not be easy to take. The oppressed person could be surprised to be asked such a question.

Initially he may respond, "Yes, you did injure me. You injured my people. You injured my race. You didn't have to do that, but you did it." Be prepared for a negative response initially from the person. As we are considerate to listen, the second level of bricks comes down from the wall. Slowly it begins to fall.

The next level is removed by experiencing together the *critical moment*. In this step the initiator and the respondent take a hard look at their relationship and where it got off track. The initiator admits his failures and asks for forgiveness. The hurt person either forgives the person or sets down conditions for change.

When you reach this critical moment in your relationship, then another level of the wall breaks down. Only two additional steps remain to raze it completely.

You must *cement* the relationship. Sometimes this sealing of the relationship comes with a handshake or a hug from the injured party. If the injury to the other person involves a lot of details then you might have to write down the details of how your relationship can continue. Through whatever course of action you take, you seal or cement the relationship, and another layer in the wall comes down.

The wall has been greatly reduced. Step by step and brick by brick, the barrier between you and another person has been lowered. All that remains is one layer and that layer is broken down through *continuation* or *continuity*. How will your relationship continue to grow and improve? What sort of ongoing contact will you have with this person? Devise a plan for a continued relationship.

FIVE STEPS IN ACTION

I've reduced the process of breaking down walls into five steps. But has anyone accomplished these steps successfully? How does it work out in practicality? Let's look at an example.

At the 1990 Promise Keepers conference Coach Bill McCartney was with 4,200 men in the basketball arena at the University of Colorado.

Coach Mac had completed his talk and went to sit down. The Spirit of the Lord said to him, "Look out at the audience and tell Me what you see."

He looked around the arena and said, "Father, I praise You. I thank You for the men."

Then the Spirit of the Lord said, "Look again at the color of men." Coach Mac looked out and saw a sea of white faces. "If you don't reach your brothers of color then at next year's meeting when you come, I will not be here in My glory."

When Coach Mac received this word from God, his heart became sensitive to the needs of racial reconciliation and the needs of men of color. (*Men of color* refers to any nonwhite.)

Coach Mac could answer like the apostle Paul, "I was not disobedient to the heavenly vision" (Acts 26:19). In his heart he heard the call and committed his life to the work of racial reconciliation. His heart grew with the first step of action — *compassion*.

Then Coach Mac began to convey his vision for reconciliation to those in the leadership of this men's organization and eventually to a broader group of men. The organization made a commit-ment to seek men of color to join their group. At the beginning of this book I told how Coach Mac and other leaders from Promise Keepers came to my church. They asked me to join their group, but they didn't know how I would react.

At the meeting they moved into the next step and *considered* my response. It wasn't what they expected. I said, "What do you mean coming down here in my part of the city? You've come into the community you injured by dishonoring a young football player. You injured a community that had gotten excited about a good player and a good team, but now you've suspended him. We don't like it, and we're trying to see what we can do to let you know we don't like it." I gave my response and Coach considered it.

The *critical moment* came when Coach Mac began to tell me about what led to the suspension. As he detailed the rules which were in place, Coach denied that the decision was based on prejudice or discrimination.

Then Coach saw the unbelieving look on my face, and he reflected more about what he was say-ing. He realized that behind the suspension was some prejudicial actions against African American players. The way the city and the university police exercised their rules and laws, black players were arrested in abundance while white players weren't arrested at the same rate.

The critical moment came for Coach as he acknowledged the reality of the real or perceived injury. As Coach and I have looked back at this critical moment, we saw that the Spirit of the Lord did a work in both our hearts.

The Lord showed me that my African American community and I had acted in an emotional and a prejudging manner based on the fact that the coach was a white man and the young football player was a black man. For our part, we didn't allow for rules and regulations governing the suspension. This critical moment not only brought a review in the heart of the coach (the oppressor) but also in my heart (the oppressed).

Coach and I came away from that critical moment with a vow for action. We repented to each other. Coach repented for not looking into the rules to see how they could be prejudiced against African American players. I repented for not allowing for a set of rules and operating procedures under which Coach was working. This critical moment involved each of us reflecting on our own thoughts and feelings.

At that point we began to *cement* the relationship with our own personal repentance. We asked each other for forgiveness and received it. We affirmed each other's integrity. It was the beginning point for our relationship.

The *continuation* or *continuity* of our relationship is active today. Coach Mac and the leadership of Promise Keepers offered me a seat on the board of directors. I continued the relationship by my belief in their program and my desire to serve them as brothers in Christ.

First I had to answer to the African American community and get their approval and consent to join this fast-growing men's organization. Eventually the African American community understood the motives and goals of this group and gave me permission to join the board of directors. The continuity didn't happen instantly, but it was a gradual, steady process.

Today Coach Mac and I meet together often. We pray for each other and stand in support of each other — not only when we are together, but also when we're apart. I know I can count on Bill to cover my back, and he can count on me to cover his back. When I'm with a group of African Americans, out of his presence, Coach knows that I'm not going to shoot him down. Likewise, when he is with a group of whites I know Coach is not going to shoot me down.

We also communicate through notes and cards that affirm each other. But as in any relationship we don't always agree on every point. Yet we've come to know the depth of the other's heart and his integrity. The relationship continues despite occasional disagreement. We've taken the steps to tear down the walls between us.

One of the means that Promise Keepers promotes for breaking down walls is small groups of men. It's a place for every man to be relational and vulnerable in his sharing.

Since I have been on the board of directors a group of men invited me to be a part of their small group. Initially I wondered, *What in the world is this all about? Why should I be a part of this small group? What are these guys after?* In fact, this group invited both of the African Americans on the board of directors to join their group — Dick Clark and myself.

I was very cautious and told them, "Guys, I'm not sure if I want to be a part of your small group. I'm not sure I want to be vulnerable and transparent with you." But because we needed to be in a group, and I didn't have a group, I went ahead and tried it for a little while. Deep inside I didn't have much confidence that I would be a part of it for long.

"I just want to be up front with you about my feelings," I told these men. "Then if you think I'm holding back for some reason, you'll know why."

They said, "That's OK. We know it takes time, and we're willing to wait and go through it."

So we started a tremendous journey, and I've been with this group for three years. We try to meet every week on Tuesday mornings around 8 A.M. We have coffee and share a word for the day. The group began with seven and now includes five men. Several of the men moved to other parts of the cities so they aren't a part of our group any longer.

The group has been a good experience for me, and I've learned to trust these men. We've come to know each other's families and wives as well as the individual challenges each man faces.

For example, this group has been challenging me about my weight and losing some pounds. Their honest encouragement has been a boost to me. The men are from various denominations and parts of Denver, so together we're learning how to break down the walls between us and become transparent.

At first I was skeptical about the role of this small group, but now the continuity and relationships are important in my life. It's not easy at first. We take a risk in lowering our walls and becoming transparent. Yet as we work through the five steps — compassion, consideration, critical moment, cementing and continuity — we find rich, unexpected rewards, and we continue to break down more walls.

POINTS TO PONDER

1. Compassion is the first step in letting the walls fall down. Many scriptures in the book of Matthew show the compassion Jesus had for others. Take time to study the following verses: 9:36; 14:14; 18:27; 18:33 and 20:34.

   ✓ How are you growing in compassion for others?

   ✓ How are you developing a compassion for those around you?

2. Consideration is a developed skill. As we give consideration to others, we listen to their concerns.

   ✓ Are you prepared to listen to the other person when he shares his pain?

   ✓ Evaluate your level of consideration, then develop a plan for increasing this skill.

3. The critical moment occurs when you and the other person evaluate where your relationship went off track.

   ✓ Is there someone in your life with whom you need to have a critical moment? Possibly it is in the area of race, denomination or some other area that is a wall in your life. Take the first step, move toward this critical moment and tear down this wall.

4. Cement glues our relationships together.

   ✓ Is there a relationship in your life that needs some cement?

   If someone comes to mind when you read the previous question, write down that person's name. Then purpose to put cement into that relationship.

5. Continuity or continuation is the final level of relationship that breaks down the walls completely. Developing an attitude of appreciation and gratitude is a critical part of maintaining a relationship.

   ✓ How have you modeled continuity in a relationship?

   If you can't think of any answer immediately, maybe a friend who models continuity will come to mind. Make an effort this week to write or call that friend and express appreciation for the continuity.

6. I used the example of Coach McCartney and how we walked through this five-step process of tearing down the walls.

   ✓ Have you had some successes at tearing down the walls in your life?

   ✓ Have you gone through this process from start to finish?

   If so, make some notes about it and share

it with a friend. The fact that you've started the journey will be an encouragement to you and the friend.

Possibly through reading this chapter you've thought of a wall in your life which needs to be torn down. Plan a course of action, starting with step one and continuing through to the continuity stage. Record your progress at each step as the wall is torn down. The record will be an encouragement to continue breaking down the walls.

7. You'll recall my skepticism about the importance of a small group and in particular the group I joined. Yet I didn't hide my skepticism from the other men.

✓ Are you in a small group?

✓ Do you know a group of men who could start a group or an existing group you could possibly join?

If you are in a group, think of ways to deepen your relationship with the other men and become more transparent in your meetings together. Your risk might be the first step toward developing this deeper relationship.

CHAPTER 8

BREAKING DOWN THE WALLS FOR COUPLES

Reconciliation. So far I've use the word to talk about issues of race or denominations. Yet reconciliation applies to many other areas and relationships. Through forty years of marriage to my lovely bride, Edgar Lee, I have seen how walls go up and come down within a marriage relationship.

Our story together starts in the segregated climate of the Southeastern United States in the 1930s and 1940s. I lived in a small Oklahoma town with all the evidences and trappings of segregation. To add insult to injury in those days, there were different classes of Negroes. In my case I was the son of a part-time pastor who had ten children and meager means.

Among the other Negroes was a man named Mr. Moye. He had carved out a fairly lucrative job at the prestigious Oxford Hotel as the night bell captain. At that time Oklahoma was a dry state, and alcoholic beverages were illegal. Mr. Moye gained considerable financial security by acquiring illegal liquors and other favors for the guests — particularly the male guests. From his earnings Mr. Moye was able to provide a more-than-decent living experience for his wife and eight children.

As a youngster I created a set of values in my mind to help me cope with my family's economic pressures. I thought anyone who didn't follow these values was not walking and living after the Spirit of God. Since I didn't have material possessions, I chose to value spiritual possessions on a higher level. It was common for me to think, *I'm going to heaven, but the Moye family is bound for hell.* I realize these were strong words, but they were my coping mechanism for not having much materially.

I later learned that one time early in the morning Mr. Moye observed my father going to work with his children, including me. He said to his daughter, "Do you reckon the Reverend Porter is really taking those little kids to work with him?" Mr. Moye saw the work ethic in our family firsthand.

In the years to come Mr. Moye and his family joined the little Holiness church where I grew up as the minister's son. Though I was aware of the Moye family at the church I didn't give them much thought. Although they gave their lives to the Lord and were well behaved, I had this barrier in my mind and heart toward them. A bit of pride swelled inside as I thought, *Our family has the upper hand in the realm of the spirit. You are a Johnny-come-lately and not on my level.*

When I was nineteen years old, I discovered Edgar Lee Moye, the object of my affections and the girl of my dreams. I realized she was the girl the Lord had shown me in a vision at the age of twelve. Many people don't believe in the reality of dreams, but I have found that some dreams have strengthened my relationship with the Lord.

I had a sweet period in my walk with Christ from age nine through age thirteen in which the Lord gave me many dreams and visions. In one particular instance I saw myself as a middle-aged man driving up to a church in a good-sized black car. As I climbed out of the car, I looked across the car seat and saw the woman who was obviously my wife get out on the other side. She was tall, honey complexioned and moved with elegance.

I was confronted with the reality that the daughter of this gentleman who worked at the local hotel was the girl in my dream. The pull of Lee's own person and her attractiveness was greater than any financial barrier. After a nine-month courtship I asked her to marry me, and she agreed. Our city-wide newspaper announced our wedding with an integrated wedding party, which was an unusual event for a young African American couple in this

Southern city. With her family's help we were able to set up our new household.

I was in my junior year of college at Phillips University, and we didn't have a lot of money. Together we made out our grocery list. For many years I had shopped, and I felt like I was a good shopper buying food for the ten children in our family. Lee and I had our accounting right down to the last penny.

On the shopping list were pork chops. As the shopper I selected the items on the list and brought them home. As Lee unpacked the bags, I went to my desk in the living room and began to study for my classes.

I could hear Lee unpacking the groceries. She exclaimed, "What is this junk?"

My initial thoughts were, *What is she calling junk? I bought the groceries, and I didn't buy any junk!*

Then Lee called into the living room and said, "Phillip, what is this? Where are my pork chops?"

I walked into the kitchen and said, "What do you mean, where are your pork chops? Those are your pork chops!"

"This isn't a pork chop! What is this stuff?"

Our two backgrounds clashed. My family bought thinly cut porked steak. We fried it until it was crisp and used the drippings to make gravy. We took our porked steak and stretched it for the whole family.

Lee's family was accustomed to buying center cut pork chops that were thick and juicy. They stuffed these pork chops with applesauce, bread dressing or rice and made their meal around them. In Lee's mind, when she made out the list, she pictured that type of pork chop. I pictured something completely different.

We had our first argument over these pork chops. That night Lee went home to her mother's and spent the night with her family. During the first month of our marriage this incident highlighted a critical difference in our value system and backgrounds. I realized we had a wall or barrier in our expectations and relationship. Her family was used to finer material possessions than my family.

Through the years I like to tell people that we've had to work out a number of things in our relationship. In material things Lee has brought me to a higher level, but in spiritual matters I've brought her to a higher level. With tongue in cheek I say that over the years I've given her eight children so she could learn to love pork steak and stretching the dollar. She taught me to love pork chops stuffed with apples or dressing!

We learned to blend our backgrounds together. As a result we broke down the walls in our relationship to become one flesh. Without Lee's input I probably would not have valued the dollar very much because my value system was based on the spiritual realm and the world to come. Initially I didn't give a lot of attention to amassing the things that we needed materially. And I've shared with her the values and objectives of a spiritual relationship with God.

BREAK DOWN THE WALLS BETWEEN COUPLES

Back when I first married no one who knew me would have said I had a prejudiced bone in my body. In fact, I thought I was a consummate reconciler and integrator and extender of self. It took the Holy Spirit to convict me and show me clearly that I had prejudged others.

I define prejudice as any action toward other people done out of ignorance. It doesn't have to be racial, but it can be within a race, a denomination or a group of people. Each of us needs to seek God's wisdom and purge our hearts when prejudice creeps into our lives and relationships.

God's Word contains a beautiful description of a love relationship for couples. Biblical scholars have acclaimed the Song of Solomon as a vivid picture of God's love for mankind. Beyond the symbolic meaning of this book couples can celebrate their love relationship in this story about two lovers.

When it comes to breaking down the walls in our relationships with our spouses, a particularly relevant section is Song of Solomon 2:8-15. The Shulamite is speaking saying:

> The voice of my beloved! Behold, he comes leaping upon the mountains, skipping upon the hills. My beloved is like a gazelle or a young stag. Behold, he stands behind our wall; He is looking through the windows, gazing through the lattice.
>
> My beloved spoke, and said to me: "Rise up, my love, my fair one, come away. For

lo, the winter is past, and the rain is over and gone. The flowers appear on the earth; The time of singing has come, and the voice of the turtledove is heard in our land. The fig tree puts forth her green figs, and the vines with the tender grapes give a good smell. Rise up, my love, my fair one, and come away!"

O my dove, in the clefts of the rock, in the secret places of the cliff, let me see your face, let me hear your voice; For your voice is sweet, and your face is lovely. Catch us the foxes, the little foxes that spoil the vines, for our vines have tender grapes.

This section shows walls which have built up and which held back the beloved from his spouse. The beloved had bounced over mountains, but he could not leap over a wall (see v. 9). The beloved is strong but never uses force. The lover must come out from behind her wall and willingly venture into the openness of springtime.

We can attempt to express love and concern to our spouses, but if there are walls in our relationship (emotional, spiritual or physical), we can't leap over the walls. Instead we must work to remove bricks and lower walls.

POINTS TO PONDER

1. Marriage is an important relationship.

   ✓ What level of priority do you place your marriage?

   Sometimes work or a hobby or another friend will take a greater priority than marriage. Sometimes children interfere with the development and growth of a marriage relationship — when parents have their priorities out of line. Take a few minutes and evaluate your marriage.

   ✓ Is there a wall in your relationship?

   ✓ If so, how could you take some steps of growth to tear down this wall?

2. I give the illustration of different backgrounds between my wife and me. Different backgrounds can cause a wall in any relationship.

   ✓ Are you facing one of these walls with a family member or coworker?

   ✓ If so, how can you begin tearing down this wall?

3. The Song of Solomon is a beautiful picture of relationships. Take some time this week and read through the entire book. Since it is short, most people can read through the book in one sitting. As you

read, watch the relationship between the beloved and his lover.

✓ Take notes while reading about how the lover woos and courts the beloved.

✓ How can you apply these lessons in your own marriage or life?

CHAPTER 9

BEYOND THE COLORADO BORDER

Thousands of men across America have signed personal and individual commitments to be godly men. For this book the sixth promise of a Promise Keeper is particularly relevant — a commitment to reach beyond any racial and denominational barriers to demonstrate the power of biblical unity.

But this commitment will be impossible to keep without a foundation of honoring Jesus Christ through worship, prayer and obedience to God's

Word in the power of the Holy Spirit.

God's Spirit awakens us to inconsistency in our lives — whether it is with our wives or members of another denomination or race. The problem among the races in America has to be dealt with in much the same way as the sin problem in America — on an individual basis, one life at a time.

BEYOND MY IMAGINATION

Breaking down the walls of denominations, race and other barriers has been a key part of my life message. My involvement with Promise Keepers has broadened my opportunity beyond my imagination or dreams.

March 1995 launched the first major conference of the year in Detroit, Michigan. The PK team selected me to give the opening welcome. This particular weekend more than seventy thousand people gathered in the home of the Detroit Lions.

As I walked up to the microphone, it was evident that the tone for the year needed to be set in appreciation to God. I was thankful for the opportunity to come before men from all over the nation and bring the message of salvation, integrity and reconciliation.

Just before I spoke I asked God to put the words in my mouth. After the initial, "Good evening, gentlemen," I said, "We must admit this stadium is an awesome place and this is a memorable night. We have all gathered here where many great Detroit Lion football players have done their best to bring joy and excitement to hundreds of thousands of fans over the years. Tonight we are thrilled to know that we have been called of God to come and present to you not the Lions but the Lion of the tribe of Judah." Then I led them in prayer. To me and those in attendance we struck a chord to begin a year of lifting up Jesus.

BREAKING DOWN THE INTERNATIONAL WALLS

Beyond our borders in the United States the walls also need to fall down. In early February 1996 I was privileged to join a team of men on a trip to South Africa.

On the way we stopped briefly in London, England. Several men from Ireland and Great Britain met with us. Despite the long-term conflict between Protestants and Catholics in Ireland, these brothers were interested in starting men's groups in their countries.

At one of the old, stately gentleman's clubs in London, we had lunch with these brothers. God is planting seeds of reconciliation across the globe. We have continued to listen to their needs and have ongoing discussions about how we can help facilitate the program in these other countries.

After only a few hours in London our team departed for South Africa. Pastor Ray McCauley from the Rhema Church in Johannesburg met us. Pastor Ray leads a five-thousand-member, multi-racial church which has been active in breaking down the racial walls of apartheid in his country.

Pastor Ray arranged for us to meet with F. W. de Klerk, one of the two deputy presidents of South Africa. He wanted to meet with us and affirm his commitment to racial reconciliation and the breaking down of walls between people.

This year South Africa has integrated soccer, cricket and rugby teams, and all three may capture world titles. While in South Africa I experienced an incredible sense of oneness among the people. I told de Klerk and the others, "You know, God has tremendous humor. Like James William Johnson, the great Negro poet, in his poem "Go Down Death" said, "God was sitting in His great high heaven the other day. He looked down and saw Sister Caroline. He told Death to go down to Savannah, Georgia, and get Sister Caroline and bring her back to Him."

The picturesque story of God bringing mankind to Himself is what is happening today in South Africa. The walls of apartheid are slowly coming down, but black Africans are still suffering. South African leaders who should be leading the oneness are leading the separation.

God said that He would get us men where we like to go — the cowboy stadiums, football stadiums, cricket fields and rugby fields. When they meet on Saturday for games, they'll have worship services instead. These are some of the ideas that I discussed with this South African leader.

A New Boldness for Reconciliation

In late February 1996 I flew to the nation of India with Coach Mac and his wife, Bishop Wellington Boone and his wife, Katherine, plus several others on the team. We were invited to speak at training sessions for pastors across India. During the day sessions in Visakhapatnam, about two or three thousand pastors came for the meetings. In the evenings we held evangelistic meetings which reached as many as ten thousand people at a time.

One of the strongest forces in the nation of India is the caste system. It has built a wall between different classes of people. The system is based on the belief that if you are content in your caste and don't try to rise above it, then in your next life you can rise to the next level of the caste system. In other words the entire system is based on a belief in reincarnation, which is completely contrary to the teaching of the Bible.

One day during the session Coach Mac was invited to speak to the crowd of pastors. His topic was a familiar one — reconciliation. As I've mentioned in other sections of this book, Coach has felt the pain and earned the platform to speak on this topic of prejudice. Because he spends time praying and fasting about this topic, Coach has an incredible ability to reach out and touch his audience — even when in another country like India.

Wellington Boone and I sat together in this session and listened to Coach. Suddenly I turned to Wellington and said, "I can't believe the boldness of Coach Mac. He's preaching against the caste system in India! It's so foundational to everyone's way of life here — even the Christians. I wonder how the crowd will react to this teaching."

Unlike my experience of preaching on reconciliation in an all-white church at age sixteen, no one walked out of the stadium. Everyone sat and listened attentively. Some people took notes as Coach talked and outlined a plan to break down this strong wall of the caste system.

Afterward, through a question and answer session, some of the pastors gave a reaction to Coach Mac's message. Every comment was positive! One pastor said, "You're right, Coach. We've been wrong not to face this stronghold or wall in our culture. We need to follow Christ and not our culture." Another man promised, "We're going to take this message back to our congregations and see how the Spirit of God moves."

The impact of such a message is difficult to measure, but from the response, I believe the Spirit of God is moving across India from Coach's message. These shepherds are taking the message of hope and reconciliation to their respective congregations.

We left India with a renewed sense of hope and a vision for seeing cracks in some of the walls. The wall of the caste system is beginning to fall down. We praised God for the chance to minister and spread the message of reconciliation to India.

A Shared Vision

The vision of reconciliation and a ministry to men in particular was born as God sowed these ideas in the hearts of men. Several men caught this new vision from God. In South Africa Peter Pollack, F. W. de Klerk and Ray McCauley were among these men.

Peter Pollack is one of the greatest cricket players in South Africa. One day several years ago Peter was talking with his pastor about the condition of his country. He said, "It would be nice if the cricket fields could be used for rallies for Jesus Christ." Peter caught a vision for the soccer, rugby and cricket stadiums of his country to be filled with men praising God. At that time there was no Promise Keepers organization in the United States and no movement of men toward racial reconciliation. Peter was sensitive to the heart of God, and the seed of a vision was planted in his heart.

On the other side of the world, almost six years ago at the University of Colorado, Coach Bill McCartney had a similar vision. He wanted to fill the football stadiums of his country with men who would stand for integrity. The seed of a vision was planted in Coach Mac's heart for what eventually became this group called Promise Keepers.

When people share similar ideas on opposite sides of the world, some would call that coincidence. Because we believe in the power of God's Spirit and His direction for our lives, there are no coincidences. There are only God-directed actions from His people.

God is the great Sower. Through Christ the Father reconciled the world to Himself. He wants those who know God to live out this vision of reconciliation.

Jesus talked about seeds and harvest as a metaphor. In Matthew 9:37-38 He said, "The harvest truly is plentiful, but the laborers are few. Therefore pray the Lord of the harvest to send out laborers into His harvest."

In the next chapter of Matthew, Jesus called the disciples and sent them out to preach the good news about Him. The disciples were sent in pairs. As they went the men were filled with experiences and knowledge of their time with Jesus Christ. These men prayed about working in the harvest field of souls. They became the answer to their prayers through their actions.

Toward the end of His life on earth Jesus prayed for His disciples and then all believers:

> And the glory which You gave Me I have given them, that they may be one just as We are one: I in them, and You in Me; that they may be *made perfect in one*, and that the world may know that You have sent Me, and have loved them as You have loved Me (John 17:22-23, italics added).

Through this prayer Jesus planted a seed of an idea — that the walls which separate people will fall down and people would be made perfect in one.

Now as we pray that prayer of unity, the walls are beginning to come down around the globe.

Here's how the vision has grown between Dave Wardel and Bill McCartney. In 1989 these two men began to pray for unity and a men's movement. The Promise Keepers movement has grown in leaps and bounds. Just look at the statistics:

1989	two men
1990	72 men
1991	4,200 men
1992	22,500 men
1993	50,000 men
1994	320,000 men
1995	725,000 men
1996	possibly 1,400,000 men

166

God is multiplying the seed of reconciliation and breaking down walls across the world.

Recently I met with a group of black leaders from New York City. These men flew across the nation to Denver so they could meet with some of the leaders from Promise Keepers. One of them told me, "We're just bowled over by Promise Keepers. These white men are openly repenting to black men. These men want forgiveness." We talked about the recent changes in various denominations.

The Pentecostal Fellowship of North America made an open statement of repentance in late 1994. Leaders made a call for healing among the black and white races and stated that the PFNA had allowed separation between white and black Pentecostals go on for too long. Now an African American man leads that group.

In the summer of 1995 Southern Baptist leaders in the same spirit of reconciliation openly repented and denounced racism as a deplorable sin. They acknowledged their sin of condoning slavery during the civil war and of opposing the civil rights movement.

God is at work in the hearts of men. Coach Mac and a team of PK men made a sweep through the eastern part of the United States recently, speaking to different African American groups and pastors.

Coach says, "We must reach out and touch the pain. I repent for myself, my brothers and my nation. I love you, brother, and I'm sorry." His attitude has become contagious across the nation. When African American men and men of other races see this attitude, it consumes them. What comes from the heart reaches the heart.

As I was talking with one of these men from New York he exclaimed, "We've never seen anything like this!" A young seminary student in the group told me, "We've always been told to forget the man [the man in power or the white man]. But this guy got my heart. I had to come out here and see if this thing is for real."

Instead of forgetting the man we need to break down the walls between us and work together.

Nathan the prophet went to David the king to tell him a story about a man in the kingdom who had many possessions. This man took a little lamb which was the only possession of another man. David responded, "As the Lord lives, the man who has done this shall surely die!" (2 Sam. 12:5).

Then Nathan turned to David and said, "You are the man!" (v. 7). He reminded David of how he took Uriah's wife, Bathsheba.

For the African American, "the man" is the man with power and possibilities. From an early age we are taught to "forget the man," to "forget the white man." That man with power has introduced crack into our neighborhoods and turned our kids into junkies. That man has kept us in poverty and hasn't allowed us to have an education and opportunities in the world. So we say, "Forget the man. We're going to do our own thing."

But we can't forget the man. Through the example of many godly men, the hearts of the African American community are softened in a new way. Coach Mac and others aren't just saying they are sorry for the wrong done across racial lines; they are daily putting their words into practice.

Instead of forgetting the man, African Americans, like the leaders from New York, are drawn to come to Denver and meet with white men. They've learned that they cannot forget the man. Through soft and sensitive hearts, the walls are beginning to tumble in our nation and in our world

POINTS TO PONDER

1. Make some notes about your growth in each of these areas: worship, prayer and obedience to God's Word in the power of the Holy Spirit.

    ✓ How are you honoring Jesus Christ through worship, prayer and obedience to God's Word in the power of the Holy Spirit?

    ✓ Is there room for improvement?

    ✓ What steps can you take to grow?

2. Coach Mac models a boldness to tear down the wall of prejudice. The story about India showed me again the courage that Coach has acquired in this area.

    ✓ How can you learn from his example?

    ✓ How can you begin the journey of tearing down this wall in your own life?

    ✓ Read Acts 4:13,29-31. What do these verses say about boldness?

    Ponder steps you could take; then with new courage move ahead.

3. Consider how God awakened a shared vision for reaching men around the world. The seeds of ideas were planted in the hearts of men in South Africa and the

United States — at about the same time period.

✓ What vision does this give you for the larger picture of God's concern and movement in today's world?

Take several minutes and spend it thanking God for His sovereign hand in our lives.

4. I tell the story about the New York leaders who met with us in Denver. They saw something unique happening through a broad-based movement of godly men. Through sensitive hearts the walls of prejudice are falling down.

✓ How can you foster a new sensitivity to the walls in your life and then work to tear down those walls?

CHAPTER 10

ONE BRICK AT A TIME

I t's an ancient riddle with a simple answer. How do you eat an elephant? It looks completely overwhelming for any person to eat an entire elephant. The size and volume are too much. Where does a person start? The answer is simple. You eat an elephant one bite at a time.

The same overwhelming feelings arise when we consider topics like prejudice and reconciliation. You may wonder where to begin. Maybe you think the walls are too high between different denominations, races and people. We need to ask ourselves, "How can we tear down these walls?"

In my lifetime I've seen many changes. The days of "whites only" signs and segregated restrooms and eating places have disappeared in this country. We've made progress toward reconciliation and equality.

But some of the walls still exist, and they're as solid as ever.

Let's consider economic wealth. There is immense inequality in terms of education, economic earning power and possessions among white Americans and African Americans or any other racial groups.

We've made strides toward tearing down denominational walls. Instead of emphasizing our church affiliation we are turning to emphasize the Lord Jesus Christ. We are now trying to focus on our common beliefs rather than putting so much emphasis on our differences. These walls are coming down, but it hasn't been without controversy, pain and discussion.

Consider the amazing transformation of South Africa, a country which has been steeped in tradition and apartheid. Or consider the new openness we sensed during our recent trip to India. I continue to marvel at the boldness of Coach McCartney to preach against the caste system in India — and to have his teaching accepted from the Christian leadership. The walls are beginning to fall down.

The task may seem overwhelming and impossible, but we can take down these walls one brick at a time. We may scratch our hands in the process. There will be pain. As we commit ourselves to

God's work in our lives, we'll see hearts changed as people follow God's steps.

The journey of a thousand miles begins with a single step. None of us can change the world unless we try.

My hope and dream as you've read these pages is that you've been given new tools for breaking down walls. I hope my stories and personal struggles with reconciliation have inspired you not to turn bitter in the struggle but to seek God's direction and wisdom for your life. Ask the Lord how you can break down walls. As we are stirred into action, God can use our lives for His glory in the work of reconciliation.

HOW TO USE THE STUDY GUIDE QUESTIONS

Throughout this book you will discover personal application for your own journey toward reconciliation — across races, denominations or in your marriage.

Each chapter of *Let the Walls Fall Down* contains material for your personal growth in a section called "Points to Ponder." These questions at the end of each chapter help you apply the stories and teaching to your life. Change won't happen overnight but requires careful planning and thought.

This appendix will help you use the questions for either discussion within a small group or individually. While this guide can be used for individual study, ideally the guide is designed for study within the context of a small group. A small group provides essential elements for spiritual growth — accountability, discipline and authenticity. We need to gather around us other people whom we trust for their love and encouragement.

Before using the discussion questions, here are some steps to consider:

- *Prepare.* The questions are directly from the context of each chapter. Before working through the questions read or reread the chapter.

- *Select a leader (in a group context).* It's rare that dynamics in a group work properly unless someone is appointed the leader. Select someone with leadership and discernment skills. The leader will guide the discussion, make sure the group stays on relevant subjects and provide everyone an opportunity to participate. The leader isn't expected to lecture to the group but to promote discussion and interaction between the participants.

- *Probe for honest answers.* A key ingredient for honest answers is to take time for reflection or looking deep within. Remove any masks or self-doubt and look deep inside yourself.

- *Keep confidentiality.* "What is said here stays here." Confidentiality is a critical ingredient so members of the group feel comfortable to reveal their deepest feelings. If this is violated then it has a lasting impact on the group.

- *Promote consistent attendance.* The chapters in *Let the Walls Fall Down* build on each other in terms of concepts. Consistent attendance should be encouraged. Instead of a commitment to the entire study, secure a commitment for four weeks. Then during the fourth week discuss the group dynamics and secure a commitment from the group for five additional weeks to complete the book.

- *Encourage accountability.* Whether you work through this book in a group or as an individual, make a point to have one person as an accountability partner. This person will help "hold your feet to the fire" of accountability. Seek a person who will allow you to be honest yet not judge you. Despite setting high expectations and goals for ourselves, each of us falls short. But if someone else holds us accountable, when we fall off the horse, we can get back on again. Give this person permission to ask questions about your growth progress. Often such a relationship is the difference between simply reading the material and applying it in your daily life.

- *Seek the guidance of the Holy Spirit.* This point is for Christian readers. As you work through this book, try to balance structure of the questions and spontaneity. Give yourself permission not to answer every question or follow every assignment. Each reader and each group have a different set of circumstances and dynamics. Some questions will stir intense discussion and interest while others will not be relevant. Give yourself permission to move through the book at your own pace. At the same time seek God's guidance through His Holy Spirit as you work through each chapter.

- *Write down your answers to the questions and assignments.* An old Chinese proverb says, "He who writes tastes life twice." As you work through the "Points to Ponder," use a yellow legal pad or your computer to record your answers to the questions. More than simply mentally answering these questions, the writing process will allow for deeper life reflection. Writing down the answers will show concretely your commitment to discover answers for your life. Also your written pages will give a record of your commitments and discoveries. As the weeks and months pass you can return to your written answers. They will benchmark your progress. The journey begins with a commitment to write down the answers.

ATTENTION PASTORS
AND GROUP LEADERS

Order *Let the Walls Fall Down* for your church or
men's group. Wholesale discounts are available.

Call 1-800-283-8494

or contact:

Creation House
600 Rinehart Road
Lake Mary, FL 32746
Phone: 407-333-3132
Fax: 407-333-7129
web site: http:// www.strang.com

If you enjoyed *Let the Walls Fall Down,* we would like
to recommend the following books:

101 Promises Worth Keeping
by Neil Eskelin

Reading these promises daily will challenge you to make
a commitment to secure your relationships with others
and anchor your future. In a world filled with shattered
vows and broken hearts, you will encounter *101 Promises
Worth Keeping.*

The Key to Everything
by Jack Hayford

When you hear the word *give,* do you want to run the
other way? Jack Hayford will teach you that giving at the
right time, in the right spirit and for the right reasons is
the key to everything.

Strong Men in Tough Times
by Edwin Louis Cole

"What you believe is the basis for conduct, character and
destiny," says author Ed Cole. Men have lost the meaning of manhood in their quest for self-gratification with
the world progressing technologically, but regressing
morally and spiritually. While the world looks for better
methods, God looks for better men.

If you would like to order any of these titles, please
contact a sales representative at:

Creation House
600 Rinehart Road
Lake Mary, FL 32746
Phone: 800-283-8494
Web site: http://www.strang.com